TRADITION, CONFLICT, AND MODERNIZATION

Perspectives on the American Revolution

Historical Monument of the American Republic, a gigantic painting (9 feet, 3 inches high by 13 feet, 1 inch wide; oil on canvas) by Erastus Salisbury Field (1805–1900), completed in 1876. [The Morgan Wesson Memorial Collection in the Museum of Fine Arts, Springfield, Massachusetts.]

TRADITION, CONFLICT, AND MODERNIZATION

Perspectives on the American Revolution

Edited by

RICHARD MAXWELL BROWN
University of Oregon
Eugene, Oregon

DON E. FEHRENBACHER
Stanford University
Stanford, California

Academic Press New York   San Francisco   London
A Subsidiary of Harcourt Brace Jovanovich, Publishers

This is a volume in

STUDIES IN SOCIAL DISCONTINUITY

A complete list of titles in this series appears at the end of this volume.

ACADEMIC PRESS, INC.
111 Fifth Avenue, New York, New York 10003

United Kingdom Edition published by
ACADEMIC PRESS, INC. (LONDON) LTD.
24/28 Oval Road, London NW1

Library of Congress Cataloging in Publication Data

Main entry under title:

Tradition, conflict, and modernization.

    (Studies in social discontinuity)
    Revised papers presented at a Bicentennial conference
held at the Institute of American History, Stanford
University, July 15-16, 1976.
    Includes index.
    1.   United States—History—Revolution, 1775-1783—
Historiography—Congresses.   I.   Brown, Richard Maxwell.
II.   Fehrenbacher, Don Edward,   Date   III.   Stanford
University.   Institute of American History.   IV.   Series.
E209.T83   1977   973.3'07'2   77-14259
ISBN 0—12—137650—8

Contents

II THE PERSPECTIVE OF CONFLICT

III THE PERSPECTIVE OF MODERNIZATION

List of Contributors

Richard Maxwell Brown (1, 73) (B.A., Reed College; A.M. and Ph.D., Harvard University), formerly professor at the College of William and Mary, is Beekman Professor of Northwest and Pacific History at the University of Oregon and in the summer of 1976 was Visiting Coe Professor of American History at Stanford University. His publications include *The South Carolina Regulators* (1963); *Anglo-American Political Relations, 1675–1775* (1970), co-edited with Alison G. Olson; and *Strain of Violence: Historical Studies of American Violence and Vigilantism* (1975).

Don E. Fehrenbacher (1) (A.B., Cornell College; A.M. and Ph.D., The University of Chicago) is Coe Professor of History and American Studies and Director of the Institute of American History at Stanford University. In 1967–1968 he was Harmsworth Professor of American History at Oxford University. His publications include *Chicago Giant: A Biography of "Long John" Wentworth* (1957); *Prelude to Greatness: Lincoln in the 1850's* (1962); and the completing and editing of *The Impending Crisis: 1848–1861* (1976) by David M. Potter, which won the Pulitzer Prize for History in 1977.

Michael Kammen (13) (A.B., George Washington University; Ph.D., Harvard University) is Newton C. Farr Professor of American History and Culture at Cornell University. His publications include *A Rope of Sand: The Colonial Agents, British Politics, and the American Revolution* (1968); *Colonial New York: A History* (1976); and *People of Paradox: An Inquiry Concerning the Origin of American Civilization* (1972), which received the Pulitzer Prize for History in 1973.

Kenneth A. Lockridge (103) (B.A., Yale University; M.A. and Ph.D., Princeton University) is Professor of History at the University of Michigan. His publications include *A New England Town: The First Hundred Years: Dedham, Massachusetts, 1636–1736* (1970) and *Literacy in Colonial New England: An Enquiry into the Social Context of Literacy in the Early Modern West* (1974).

Charles Tilly (45) (A.B. and Ph.D., Harvard University) is Professor of Sociology and History and Director of the Center for Research in Social Organization at the University of Michigan. His publications include *The Vendée: A Sociological Analysis of the Counter-Revolution of 1793* (1964); the editing of *The Formation of the National States in Western Europe* (1975); and, with Louise and Richard Tilly, *The Rebellious Century: 1830–1930* (1975).

Acknowledgments

On July 15–16, 1976, the Institute of American History of Stanford University held a Bicentennial conference on "The American Revolution in the Modern World." Chapters 2–5 of this book are revised versions of the papers read at the conference. We wish to acknowledge the contributions of the following persons: President Richard W. Lyman of Stanford, who delivered the luncheon address at the conference on July 16th; Professors George Harmon Knoles, Lewis M. Spitz, Carl Degler, and Thomas A. Bailey, who chaired the conference sessions; Betty K. Eldon, who assisted with the arrangements for the conference; and Ala Hamilton, who typed the manuscript for this book.

Williamsburg, Virginia   R. M. B.
Stanford, California   D. E. F.

January, 1977

1

Introduction

Richard Maxwell Brown
Don E. Fehrenbacher

During the past several decades, historians of the American Revolution have given much of their attention to three major problems: the intellectual character of the Revolution, its relation to the trend of modernization, and its standing as a manifestation of social conflict. Taken together, the essays in this book expand our knowledge and understanding of all three subjects.

For many years, the ideological aspect of the Revolution was relatively neglected, as historians focused primarily on the question of whether the Revolution had been truly a social upheaval. Carl Becker introduced the social issue with his resounding declaration that the Revolution involved not only the "question of home rule" but also the question of "who should rule at home." [1] In the same period, J. Allen Smith and Charles A. Beard published trenchant works picturing the adoption of the Constitution as an American Thermidor that curbed the plebeian radicalism of the Revolutionary movement. [2] The works of Becker, Beard, and

---

[1] Carl Becker, *The History of Political Parties in the Province of New York, 1760–1766* (Madison: University of Wisconsin, 1909).

[2] J. Allen Smith, *The Spirit of American Government: A Study of the Constitution: Its Origin, Influence, and Relation to Democracy* (New York: Macmillan, 1907); Charles A. Beard, *An Economic Interpretation of the Constitution of the United States* (New York: Macmillan, 1913).

RICHARD MAXWELL BROWN AND DON E. FEHRENBACHER

Smith, together with subsequent books by Arthur M. Schlesinger, Sr. and Vernon L. Parrington,[3] provided the framework for interpreting the revolutionary era as a time of social conflict in which protodemocratic forces—urban workers, political radicals, and frontier farmers—were arrayed against a reactionary coalition of upper-class merchants and planters. According to this view, the proponents of social revolution reached their peak of influence in the framing of the Articles of Confederation, a document with a pronounced bias against strong central government. Thereafter, the strength of the social revolutionaries receded to the dénouement of 1787.

The interpretation emphasizing social conflict, reinforced by Merrill Jensen in 1948 and 1950 with two impressive studies of the confederation period, reached something of a climax in a book by Elijah P. Douglass significantly titled *Rebels and Democrats: The Struggle for Equal Political Rights and Majority Rule during the American Revolution.*[4] In general, the historians who focused on social conflict tended to slight the ideas of the revolutionary leaders. The great documents of the movement were viewed essentially as propaganda pieces in the power struggle between social reactionaries and social revolutionaries.

The American emphasis on social revolution was paralleled by a trend among British historians which, from far different premises, had the same effect of depreciating the role of ideology. In two influential volumes that came out in 1929, Lewis B. Namier produced a portrait of Britain in the age of the American Revolution that resolutely omitted ideology as a meaningful force

[3] Arthur M. Schlesinger, Sr., *The Colonial Merchants and the American Revolution, 1763–1776* (New York: Columbia University, 1918) ; Vernon L. Parrington, *Main Currents in American Thought: An Interpretation of American Literature from the Beginnings to 1920; Volume One: 1620–1800, The Colonial Mind* (New York: Harcourt, Brace, 1927).

[4] Merrill Jensen, *The Articles of Confederation: An Interpretation of the Social–Constitutional History of the American Revolution, 1774–1781* (Madison: University of Wisconsin Press, 1948) and *The New Nation: A History of the United States during the Confederation, 1781–1789* (New York: Alfred A. Knopf, 1950) ; Elijah P. Douglass, *Rebels and Democrats: The Struggle for Equal Political Rights and Majority Rule during the American Revolution* (Chapel Hill: University of North Carolina Press, 1955).

2

in politics.[5] Namier's concept of the British "political nation" was restricted to a narrow political elite represented in Parliament. He characterized this elite as one swayed only by personal and family interests expressed through the material considerations of patronage, government contracts, and mercantile interest. So persuasive was Namier's argument that his many followers on both sides of the Atlantic were diverted from investigating the function of ideas in the making of the Revolution.

Thus, whether historians enlisted in the social-conflict school of Beard, Becker, and Parrington,[6] or followed the lead of Namier, the result was much the same—a relative neglect of the intellectual history of the Revolution. A reaction set in, however, during the 1950s. Clinton Rossiter, studying the ideology of the founding fathers, and Douglass Adair, chiefly interested in Jeffersonian ideology, stirred interest in the ideas of the Revolution with a stream of monographs and articles.[7] Then in 1959, Caroline Robbins turned the flank of the Namierite hostility to ideas by showing that ideology survived meaningfully in eighteenth-century Britain. Robbins explicated the "commonwealth" ideology in British political writing, an intricate complex of libertarian ideas originating in the seventeenth century. She pointed to William Pitt the elder as its most prominent exponent in Britain, but ended her richly textured study with the assertion that the commonwealth ideology reached its climax in the American Revolution.[8]

Other historians took up the challenge offered in Robbins' work, and soon there emerged the modern ideological interpre-

[5] Lewis B. Namier, *The Structure of Politics at the Accession of George III*, 2 vols. (London: Macmillan, 1929).

[6] Among many studies of conflict-oriented historians, see especially Richard Hofstadter, *The Progressive Historians: Turner, Beard, Parrington* (New York: Alfred A. Knopf, 1968).

[7] Clinton L. Rossiter, *Seedtime of the Republic: The Origin of the American Tradition of Political Liberty* (New York: Harcourt, Brace, 1953); Douglass Adair, "The Intellectual Origins of Jeffersonian Democracy" (Ph.D. dissertation, Yale University, 1943) and *Fame and the Founding Fathers*, ed. H. Trevor Colbourn (Chapel Hill: University of North Carolina Press, 1974).

[8] Caroline Robbins, *The Eighteenth-Century Commonwealthman* (Cambridge: Harvard University Press, 1959).

tation of the American Revolution.[9] It was presented most fully
in three books by Bernard Bailyn: *The Ideological Origins of the
American Revolution* (the leading general work on the subject);
Origins of American Politics (a sketch of the colonial political
culture that served as the context of the revolutionary ideology);
and *The Ordeal of Thomas Hutchinson* (a sensitive study of the
failure of loyalists, typified by Hutchinson, to understand and
cope with the revolutionary ideology).[10] With the subsequent
appearance of works by H. Trevor Colbourn, Gordon Wood, and
Pauline Maier, the ideological interpretation was established.[11]
So thoroughly and with such sophistication had the subject been
covered that there seemed little more to be said. Yet in 1975, *The
Machiavellian Moment* by J. G. A. Pocock appeared, a stunning
work in the history of political theory that pushed the origins of
the commonwealth ideology (or "country ideology," as he prefers
to call it) back to the Italian Renaissance.[12]

Although the revolutionary ideology and its origins have thus
been studied in exhaustive detail, the intellectual legacy of the
Revolution has not yet attracted similar interest.[13] Michael Kammen's contribution to this volume is therefore especially valuable.
His essay examining the significance of the Revolution in the

[9] The leading historiographic study of the ideological interpretation is Robert
E. Shalhope, "Toward a Republican Synthesis: The Emergence of an Understanding
of Republicanism in American Historiography," *William and Mary Quarterly*, 3rd
ser., 29 (1972): 48–80, citing major titles necessarily omitted in this introduction.

[10] Bernard Bailyn, *The Ideological Origins of the American Revolution* (Cam-
bridge: Harvard University Press, 1967), *Origins of American Politics* (New York:
Alfred A. Knopf, 1968), and *The Ordeal of Thomas Hutchinson* (Cambridge:
Harvard University Press, 1974).

[11] H. Trevor Colbourn, *The Lamp of Experience: Whig History and the Intellectual Origins of the American Revolution* (Chapel Hill: University of North
Carolina Press, 1965); Gordon S. Wood, *The Creation of the American Republic,
1776–1787* (Chapel Hill: University of North Carolina Press, 1969); Pauline Maier,
*From Resistance to Revolution: Colonial Radicals and the Development of Ameri-
can Opposition to Britain, 1765–1776* (New York: Alfred A. Knopf, 1972).

[12] J. G. A. Pocock, *The Machiavellian Moment: Florentine Political Thought
and the Atlantic Republican Tradition* (Princeton: Princeton University Press,
1975).

[13] But see two key works: Cecelia Kenyon, "Men of Little Faith: The Anti-
Federalists on the Nature of Representative Government," *William and Mary
Quarterly*, 3rd ser., 12 (1955): 3–43; and Richard Buel, *Securing the Revolution:
Ideology in American Politics, 1789–1815* (Ithaca: Cornell University Press, 1972).

national tradition is a stimulating invitation to further study of the subject.

Despite the recent attention to the ideology of the American Revolution, the issue of social conflict nevertheless looms large in this volume, reflecting a renewal of interest in the problem among a growing number of historians. Merrill Jensen, to be sure, never abandoned his conviction of the importance of social conflict, reiterating it in *The Founding of a Nation: A History of the American Revolution* (1968).[14] During the 1950s and 1960s, however, Jensen's was a somewhat lonely voice; for the consensus of specialists held that social conflict was a minor motif in early eighteenth-century America and the revolutionary period. As Kammen notes in his essay, this was related to a post-World War II stress on consensus by a number of leading American historians. There was also the impact of Namier, whose model of eighteenth-century politics influenced significant works on the colonies, including those of John A. Schutz on Massachusetts, David S. Lovejoy on Rhode Island, Stanley N. Katz on New York, and Lucille B. Griffith and David Alan Williams on Virginia.[15] These and other scholars dealt with a limited political scene where members of the colonial elite competed for offices and interest.

Likewise strongly challenging the social-conflict interpretation were Robert E. Brown, in his studies of dominant "middle-class democracy" in Massachusetts and Virginia, and Charles S. Sydnor, in an examination of the elite-dominated social consensus of Washington's Virginia.[16] Associated with these writings was the

14 Merrill Jensen, *The Founding of a Nation: A History of the American Revolution* (New York: Oxford University Press, 1968). See also Jensen's brief treatment, *The American Revolution within America* (New York: New York University Press, 1974).

15 John A. Schutz, *William Shirley: King's Governor of Massachusetts* (Chapel Hill: University of North Carolina Press, 1961); David S. Lovejoy, *Rhode Island Politics and the American Revolution, 1760–1776* (Providence: Brown University Press, 1958); Stanley N. Katz, *Newcastle's New York: Anglo-American Politics, 1732–1753* (Cambridge: Harvard University Press, 1968); Lucille B. Griffith, *The Virginia House of Burgesses, 1750–1774*, revised edition (University: University of Alabama Press, 1970); David Alan Williams, "Political Alignments in Colonial Virginia, 1698–1750" (Ph.D. dissertation, Northwestern University, 1959).

16 Robert E. Brown, *Middle-Class Democracy and the Revolution in Massachusetts, 1691–1780* (Ithaca: Cornell University Press, 1955) and with B. Katherine

work of Edmund S. Morgan, who, along with Helen M. Morgan, found no significant social conflict in the Stamp Act controversy. Then came Morgan's short but influential book, *The Birth of the Republic* (1956), a concise and authoritative survey of the revolutionary era from the anti-social-conflict perspective. In reply to Carl Becker's pronouncement of nearly half a century earlier, Morgan declared that although social conflict played its part in the Revolution, "to magnify the internal contest to the same proportions as the revolt against England" was to "distort it beyond recognition." [17]

Although the scholarly consensus that deemphasizes social conflict in relation to the American Revolution is far from overturned, it has recently come under strong attack. Preceded by Jesse Lemisch's studies of the radical role of seamen in the Revolutionary era,[18] an important new work appeared in the bicentennial year 1976. Bringing together the essays of a galaxy of younger historians, *The American Revolution,* edited by Alfred F. Young, describes pervasive social conflict from Boston to South Carolina.[19] Three of the contributors to our volume—Kammen, Tilly, and Brown—offer insights into the persistent issue of social conflict. None of the three asserts that such conflict was the dominant feature of the revolutionary period, but each in his own way contributes to refining the element of social conflict in that complex pattern of events called the American Revolution.

Kammen's essay shows that in the very first generation after the Revolution the debate on the legacy of the Revolution hinged,

Brown, *Virginia, 1705–1786: Democracy or Aristocracy?* (East Lansing: Michigan State University Press, 1964); Charles S. Sydnor, *Gentlemen Freeholders: Political Practices in Washington's Virginia* (Chapel Hill: University of North Carolina Press, 1958).

[17] Edmund S. and Helen M. Morgan, *The Stamp Act Crisis: Prologue to Revolution* (Chapel Hill: University of North Carolina Press, 1953); Edmund S. Morgan, *The Birth of the Republic, 1763–89* (Chicago: University of Chicago Press, 1955), especially p. 100.

[18] Jesse Lemisch, "Jack Tar vs. John Bull: The Role of New York's Seamen in Precipitating the Revolution" (Ph.D. dissertation, Yale University, 1962) and "Jack Tar in the Streets: Merchant Seamen in the Politics of Revolutionary America," *William and Mary Quarterly,* 3rd ser., 25 (1968): 371–407.

[19] Alfred F. Young, ed., *The American Revolution: Explorations in the History of American Radicalism* (De Kalb: Northern Illinois University Press, 1976).

as it has ever since, on the issue of social reform and revolution. Kammen traces our images of the Revolution through successive orientations from those of contemporaries in 1776–1799 to "realism, pluralism, and elitism" in our own time, 1945–1975. Yet, interwoven among the shifting viewpoints of generation after generation is the question first confronted by John Adams and Benjamin Rush: Were the implications of the Revolution conservative or radical? The full-fledged conservative interpretation had emerged by the 1790s in the Federalist assumption that "the Revolution was a unique and completed event whose implications had been entirely fulfilled by the creation of the American Republic." Roundly opposed was the radical view of the Jeffersonian Republicans that the Revolution was "an exemplar to oppressed peoples elsewhere, or for subsequent rebellions at home." The basic interpretative issue, according to Kammen, has continued to be whether the Revolution stands as a rationale for social stasis or as an inspiration for social change. In our own bicentennial observance, the problem was still very much with us, with conservative celebrants saluting America as it was and is, while the People's Bicentennial Commission called urgently for radical social change.[20]

Tilly, in his essay, concedes that the factor of social revolution was less important in America than in the French, Russian, and Chinese revolutions. He sees no "realignment of classes" resulting from the American Revolution. Yet he does find that the role of popular action was significantly expanded in the revolutionary period, and he analyzes that expansion by using comparative historical sociology. Comparative analysis has only rarely been employed to enhance our understanding of the American Revolution, the most notable instance being Robert R. Palmer's *The Age of the Democratic Revolution.*[21] Tilly compares local action in En-

---

[20] For a conservative critique of the People's Bicentennial Commission, see Chilton Williamson, Jr., "They Almost Stole the Bicentennial," *National Review,* August 20, 1976, pp. 898–899, 913.

[21] Robert R. Palmer, *The Age of the Democratic Revolution: A Political History of Europe and America, 1760–1800,* 2 vols. (Princeton: Princeton University Press, 1960–1965). See also, J. R. Pole, *Political Representation in England and the Origins of the American Republic* (Berkeley: University of California Press, 1971) and the works cited in Chapter 3, note 6, this volume.

7

gland and America during the decade preceding the Revolution. In doing so, he bypasses the theoretical question of social revolution to look inductively at just what the people were doing on both sides of the Atlantic. His description of "the general use of ritual, symbols, and drama in crowd action" not only increases our knowledge of the style of crowd behavior in the revolutionary period but also leads to an important general observation about "the regularity with which popular collective action consisted of ordinary people's taking over the roles and procedures of the constituted authorities." Colonial construction of extralegal parallel forms of government, says Tilly, amounted to "preparation of a genuine revolution." In a crucial way, moreover, the American Revolution was modern; for "in the means employed it stood at the leading edge of social change."

Tilly alone presents an English–American comparison, but in addition, the chapters by Tilly and Brown together offer an urban–rural comparison of revolutionary activity. Whereas Tilly focuses on the urban scene in the mother country and the colonies, Brown examines the rural scene in America. Noting the absence of social upheaval in the turbulent cities of eighteenth-century America, Brown develops the theme that whatever social revolution occurred in the revolutionary era took place primarily in the nine back-country rebellions forming the subject of his essay. Although discontented urban workers of the time lacked an ideology to inspire them to social revolution, dissident back-country farmers were led to rebel by their commitment to the "homestead ethic." Brown finds the influence of the homestead ethic spanning a long period from its origins in seventeenth-century landholding practices to its climax in the Homestead Act of 1862. In linking the homestead ethic to the nine back-country rebellions of 1740–1799, Brown does not foreclose a broader implication that the ethic played a crucial part in the decision of rural Americans to defend their farms and families in revolutionary battlefield action from Lexington and Concord to King's Mountain and Cowpens.

In more general terms, the essays by Tilly and Brown take their places in a proliferating scholarly literature concerned with urban and rural crowds and the emergence of a popular *mentalité* in the eighteenth and nineteenth centuries. Here the seminal

8

work of George Rudé, Eric J. Hobsbawm, E. P. Thompson, and Richard C. Cobb come to mind, and both Tilly and Brown have themselves made earlier contributions to this literature.[22]

The contribution of Kenneth Lockridge to this volume is oriented to still another significant trend of post–World War II scholarship—the study of modernization. Perhaps no concept in recent years has inspired more interdisciplinary work by social scientists than has modernization, and it is being used increasingly by historians to explain American history from the early eighteenth century to the era of World War I.[23] A significant new book places the Revolution squarely in the context of modernization, and a leading colonial historian has declared that the parallel process of modernization was even more important than the American Revolution itself.[24] Rooted in the new school of historical demography, which has so brilliantly enhanced our knowledge of early modern Europe and colonial America, the concept of modernization is the freshest scholarly strategy for explaining the American Revolution.

Lockridge's essay indicates that it may also turn out to be the most controversial. Expressing doubt that modernization amounted to anything more than a set of specific structural changes, he offers

22 George Rudé, *The Crowd in History: A Study of Popular Disturbances in France and England, 1730–1848* (New York: Wiley, 1964); E[dward] P. Thompson, *The Making of the English Working Class* (London: John Gollancz, 1963) and "The Moral Economy of the English Crowd in the Eighteenth Century," *Past and Present*, 50 (February 1971): 76–136; Richard C. Cobb, *The Police and the People: French Popular Protest, 1789–1820* (Oxford: Clarendon Press, 1970); Eric J. Hobsbawm and George Rudé, *Captain Swing* (New York: Pantheon, 1968); Charles Tilly, *The Vendée* (Cambridge: Harvard University Press, 1964) and (with Louise and Richard Tilly), *The Rebellious Century: 1830–1930* (Cambridge: Harvard University Press, 1975); Richard Maxwell Brown, *The South Carolina Regulators* (Cambridge: Harvard University Press, 1963).

23 The scholarly literature on modernization is enormous and still growing. In addition to works cited in the notes to Chapter 5, this volume, see Daniel Lerner, James S. Coleman, and Ronald Dore, "Modernization," in *International Encyclopedia of the Social Sciences*, ed. David L. Sills, 17 vols. (New York: Macmillan and Free Press, 1968), vol. 10, pp. 386–409.

24 Jack P. Greene, "The Social Origins of the American Revolution: An Interpretation," *Political Science Quarterly*, 88 (1973): 1–22; Richard D. Brown, *Modernization: The Transformation of American Life, 1600–1865* (New York: Hill and Wang, 1976).

the devastating suggestion that modernization is simply the "whig metaphor" in "scientific disguise." Turning more specifically to the psychological side of the concept, he asks whether modernization, as sometimes alleged, produced not only modern society but also a modern personality? His answer is a resounding "no." Yet Lockridge is by no means a traditionalist. Having written a searching study of "Social Change and the Meaning of the American Revolution," he is hospitable to the notion that the Revolution was accompanied by significant social change.[25] But it was the human response rather than the human personality, he declares, that underwent profound change in the crucible of the Revolution. Instead of a transition from "traditional" to "modern" personality, Lockridge finds an unchanging but highly adaptive personality, capable of adopting "new tactical behaviors" in response to flux and stress in the revolutionary era and in other times.

In his views on personality and modernization, Lockridge widens the focus of revolutionary interpretation to the relationship between the individual and history. The other three contributors to this volume—each in his own way—likewise offer historical insights that transcend the limits of the revolutionary era.

[25] Kenneth A. Lockridge, "Social Change and the Meaning of the American Revolution," *Journal of Social History*, 6 (1972–1973): 403–439.

I

THE PERSPECTIVE
OF TRADITION

2

The American Revolution
in National Tradition

Michael Kammen

For a long time now, observers of the American scene have remarked that we tend to be present minded and future oriented.
As Alexis de Tocqueville put it: In a democracy "the woof of
time is every instant broken, and the track of generations effaced."
One of the central themes in Erik Erikson's 1973 Jefferson Lectures, *Dimensions of a New Identity,* is that American society has
constantly been seduced by the lure of newness.[1]

One might even say, therefore, that we have had a tradition
of present mindedness, a tradition which began to be articulated
at least as early as 1789 when Jefferson wrote to Madison from
Paris that

> I set out on this ground, which I suppose to be self evident, 'that the
> earth belongs in usufruct to the living': that the dead have neither
> powers nor rights over it. . . . No society can make a perpetual consti-
> tution, or even a perpetual law. The earth belongs always to the
> living generation.[2]

[1] Alexis de Tocqueville, *Democracy in America,* ed. J. P. Mayer (Garden City:
Doubleday, 1969), p. 507; Erik Erikson, *Dimensions of a New Identity: The 1973
Jefferson Lectures in the Humanities* (New York: W. W. Norton, 1974), pp. 75–83.

[2] Thomas Jefferson to James Madison, Sept. 6, 1789, in *The Papers of Thomas
Jefferson,* ed. Julian P. Boyd (Princeton: Princeton University Press, 1958), vol. 15,

I find repetition of this resistance to the perceived tyranny of the past all through the nineteenth century. Congressman B. Gratz Brown addressed his Missouri constituents in 1850 as follows:

> With the past we have literally nothing to do, save to dream of it. Its lessons are lost and its tongue is silent. We are ourselves at the head and front of all political experience. Precedents have lost their virtue and all their authority is gone.[3]

Americans have often been concerned about their past, to be sure. Some of them have even, on occasion, been *influenced* by a sense of their history. But then our leading lights seem to come along and repudiate the "burden" of tradition. Between 1821 and 1835, for example, historical fiction about the American Revolution was immensely popular in the young United States; and during that period, the years 1826 and 1832 were regarded as dates of great commemorative significance. Yet in 1835, while Ralph Waldo Emerson was living in the Old Manse at Concord, just a few hundred yards away from "the rude bridge" he would later help to immortalize, he wrote one of his most famous essays, "Nature." Its opening sentences illustrate my point:

> Our age is retrospective. It builds the sepulchres of the fathers. It writes biographies, histories, and criticism. The foregoing generations beheld God and nature face to face; we, through their eyes. Why should not we also enjoy an original relation to the universe? Why should not we have a poetry and philosophy of insight and not of tradition, and a religion by revelation to us, and not the history of theirs?[4]

"Nature" was first published in 1836. One year later, Horace

---

pp. 384–397. See also Thomas Paine's insistence, in *The Rights of Man* (1791): "Every age and generation must be as free to act for itself, *in all cases*, as the ages and generation which preceded it. The vanity and presumption of governing beyond the grave, is the most ridiculous and insolent of all tyrannies." *The Life and Works of Thomas Paine*, ed. William M. Van der Weyde, (New Rochelle: Thomas Paine National Historical Association, 1925), vol. 6, p. 92.

[3] Quoted in Rush Welter, *The Mind of America, 1820–1860* (New York: Columbia University Press, 1975), p. 6.

[4] Ralph Waldo Emerson, "Nature," in *Nature, Addresses, and Lectures* (Boston: Houghton, Mifflin, 1885), p. 9.

Mann printed his benchmark *Prospectus for the "Common-School Journal"* and echoed Emerson with these words:

> It cannot be denied that for years past the public eye has been pointed backwards to the achievement of our ancestors, rather than forward to the condition of our posterity, as though praise of the dead fathers would provide adequately for the living sons.[5]

It appears, then, that Americans have commonly and often vocally been uneasy about tradition and its cultural weight. However, insofar as we do have an enduring sense of tradition, the American Revolution has been at its very core. The Cavalier tradition in the South, by contrast, was undermined by the shambles of Reconstruction, punctured by Thomas Jefferson Wertenbaker in 1910, and shattered by W. J. Cash in 1941.[6] The Puritan tradition, in New England and wherever New Englanders migrated, was criticized by Brooks Adams in 1887, scarified by Charles Francis Adams in 1893, and repudiated by a batch of intellectual inebriates writing under the heady influence of Freudian ferment during the 1920s.[7]

The American Revolution, however, has had a considerable and nearly continuous impact upon our national culture and literature. Unlike the Cavalier and Puritan traditions, it has never really been repudiated. The vagaries of historical revisionism have neither altered the Revolution's profoundly important place in

[5] *Life and Works of Horace Mann* (Boston: Lee and Shepard, 1891), vol. 2, pp. 4–5.

[6] See William R. Taylor, *Cavalier and Yankee: The Old South and American National Character* (New York: G. Braziller, 1961) ; Thomas Jefferson Wertenbaker, *Patrician and Plebeian in Virginia* (Princeton: Princeton University Press, 1910) and *The Planters of Colonial Virginia* (Princeton: Princeton University Press, 1922) ; W. J. Cash, *The Mind of the South* (New York: Alfred A. Knopf, 1941) , especially Book One; and Daniel Aaron, *The Unwritten War: American Writers and the Civil War* (New York: Afred A. Knopf, 1973) .

[7] See Brooks Adams, *The Emancipation of Massachusetts* (Boston: Houghton, Mifflin, 1887) ; Charles Francis Adams, *Three Episodes of Massachusetts History*, 2 vols. (Boston: Houghton Mifflin, 1893) ; Wesley Frank Craven, *The Legend of the Founding Fathers* (Ithaca: Cornell University Press, 1965) , pp. 203–207; and Ralph and Louise Boas, *Cotton Mather* (New York: Harper, 1928) .

our sense of the past nor diminished its impact in shaping our notions of nationality.[8]

Consequently, it might be useful to attempt a periodization of the American Revolution in national tradition—a kind of conjectural chronology covering the two centuries from 1776 to 1976. The periodization I offer is admittedly artificial and retrospective. It might not even be entirely recognizable to the historical participants. Nevertheless, I am convinced that it reveals some fundamental rhythms in our cultural heritage; and therefore it may have a certain utility.

I. Contemporary Speculations and Divergences, 1776–1799

What I find most interesting within the revolutionary era itself is the presence of counterpoised alternatives: varied views on the meaning and proper interpretation of the Revolution. One such divergence, for example, concerned its true chronological locus. John Adams put it this way, in a famous letter to Jefferson: "The Revolution was in the Minds of The People, and this was effected, from 1760 to 1775, in the course of fifteen Years before a drop of blood was drawn at Lexington." Benjamin Rush had quite a different perspective, which he voiced in Philadelphia in 1787: "The American War is over, but this is far from being the case with the American Revolution. On the contrary, nothing but the first act of the great drama is closed." [9]

The divergence between these two lines of interpretation is important because by 1787–1788 the Revolution had become,

---

[8] See, for example, the two fascinating charts in W. Lloyd Warner, *The Living and the Dead: A Study of the Symbolic Life of Americans* (New Haven: Yale University Press, 1959), pp. 133–134.

[9] John Adams to Jefferson, August 24, 1815, in *The Adams–Jefferson Letters*, ed. Lester J. Cappon (Chapel Hill: University of North Carolina Press, 1959), vol. 2, p. 455; Rush, *An Address to the People of the United States* (1787), in Hezekiah Niles, *Principles and Acts of the Revolution in America*, ed. Alden T. Vaughan (New York: Grosset and Dunlap, 1965), p. 334. Adams was reiterating a position he had taken ever since 1783.

16

first, a touchstone for those involved in drawing up the blueprint for a new national government and, second, a point of reference for polemicists engaged in debate over acceptance of the new Constitution. In Massachusetts, for example, one newspaper made this appeal for ratification late in 1787: "Consider that those immortal characters, who first planned the event of the revolution . . . have now devised a plan for supporting your freedom, and increasing your strength, your power and happiness." [10]

By the 1790s, owing to the intense partisanship of domestic politics as well as controversy over the relative virtues and horrors of the French Revolution, those alternative points of view articulated by Adams and Rush took on new forms that would persist for a long time. According to one position, taken especially by such New England Federalists as Fisher Ames and Timothy Dwight, the Revolution was a unique and completed event whose implications had been entirely fulfilled by the creation of the American Republic. This conservative view left little room for the Revolution as an exemplar to oppressed peoples elsewhere or for subsequent rebellions at home (such as the uprising of Daniel Shays or the Whiskey Rebellion of 1794).[11]

The opposite position, which tended to be that of the Jeffersonian Republicans—but not singularly so—received its most succinct expression later on in a letter from Jefferson to Adams: "The flames kindled on the 4th of July 1776 have spread over too much of the globe to be extinguished by the feeble engines of despotism. On the contrary they will consume those engines, and all who work them." [12] Proponents of this view perceived the Revolution as exportable and therefore meaningful overseas. Unlike the Federalists, they also regarded social and political change

[10] See Frederick R. Black, "The American Revolution as 'Yardstick' in the Debates on the Constitution, 1787–1788," *Proceedings of the American Philosophical Society*, 117 (1973): 162–185; Paul C. Nagel, *One Nation Indivisible: The Union in American Thought, 1776–1861* (New York: Oxford University Press, 1964), p. 183.

[11] See the remarks made by M. Augustus Jewett on July 4, 1840 in Terre Haute, Indiana: "This immortal declaration is due to circumstances which, in the history of a world, can never occur again . . . we are removed from the yet enduring evils of the old world." Quoted in Welter, *Mind of America*, p. 21.

[12] Jefferson to Adams, September 12, 1821, *Adams–Jefferson Letters*, vol. 2, p. 575.

at home with greater equanimity because change seemed to be an inescapable part of the legacy of 1776. For many of them the Declaration of Independence was less an historic document than a living creed.[13]

By the end of John Adams' administration, partisan politics had grown so nasty that ideological opponents could not disentangle their sense of the present from their remembrance of the past. Unable to celebrate the Fourth of July together, they held separate processions and separate dinners and heard separate orations. One characteristic toast of the day, reported in 1799, ran as follows: "John Adams—may he like Sampson slay thousands of Frenchmen, with the jawbone of Jefferson." [14]

II. Revolution Romanticized and Revolutionaries Immortalized, 1800–1832

The death of George Washington in 1799 marked the end of an era in American tradition; and the publication in 1800 of Mason Locke Weems' *Life of Washington* heralded another. The book became a fabulous best seller and had the most extraordinary impact. Many decades later, Lorenzo Sabine, first American historian of the Loyalists, looked back upon his boyhood in the beginning of the nineteenth century: "A top, a ball, a hoop, a knife, and a fishing rod, Weems's *Life of Washington* . . . *Gulliver's Travels,* and *Robinson Crusoe,* comprised every article of property which I could call my own." [15]

For two reasons, Weems inaugurated an important compo-

13 See Abraham Lincoln's "Address Before the Young Men's Lyceum of Springfield, Illinois," January 27, 1838, in *The Collected Works of Abraham Lincoln,* ed. Roy P. Basler (New Brunswick: Rutgers University Press, 1953), vol. 1, p. 112. See also Lincoln's "Temperance Address," February 22, 1842, in ibid., vol. 1, p. 278.

14 See Charles Warren, "Fourth of July Myths," *William and Mary Quarterly,* 3rd ser., 2 (1945): 261–262, 270–271.

15 Edward E. Hale, "Memoir of the Hon. Lorenzo Sabine," *Proceedings of the Massachusetts Historical Society,* 17 (1880): 372. See also William A. Bryan, *George Washington in American Literature, 1775–1865* (New York: Columbia University Press, 1952).

nent of the American tradition. First, biographies of Washington, taken together, have sold more than any other single type of historical writing in the United States. The genre runs from Weems and John Marshall to Jared Sparks and James Kirke Paulding, from Joel Headley and Washington Irving to William E. Woodward and Rupert Hughes, right on down to Douglas Southall Freeman and James T. Flexner in our own time. Second, many of these biographies were really life-and-times histories of the revolutionary era. (One wag remarked that Justice Marshall's *Washington* sold rather poorly because it had too little life and too much times.)

It is especially interesting to note that while Washington achieved instant immortality in 1800, those whom we regard today as the other founding fathers waited much longer to take their places *securely* within the pantheon: Jefferson, perhaps, with the publication of Henry Randall's three-volume biography in 1858; Franklin, possibly, with the first complete American edition of his autobiography in 1868; Adams, Hamilton, Madison, and Jay? It is hard to say just when their rights to their niches were confirmed and their contributions generally accepted and beyond cavil.

Instead, men whom we now think of as figures of secondary importance were regarded as immortals during the first quarter of the nineteenth century: John Paul Jones, whose *Life and Adventures* became a popular seller in 1807; General Francis Marion, the Swamp Fox, because of a very successful biography by Weems and Peter Horry published in 1810; Patrick Henry on account of William Wirt's fabulous biography, first brought out in 1817; James Otis and Richard Henry Lee for similar reasons during the 1820s. These men, who did not go on to have national and controversial careers after the Revolution, became the undisputed historical luminaries of the early nineteenth century. Only later, as their luster dimmed, did those whom *we* regard as members of the first rank outshine them and take their permanent places in the firmament of founders.

During these early decades of the nineteenth century, the revolutionary tradition was perpetuated by several sorts of writers other than biographers. There were the narrative histories of David Ramsay, Mercy Otis Warren, William Henry Drayton, and

Timothy Pitkin—several of them hard at work even before 1800. Despite serious attempts in recent years to resuscitate their reputations, however, their works have an antique or moldy quality—often because of a retrospective yearning for the Revolution as a golden age and, withal, a rather tendentious tone. These books certainly helped to *sustain* the Revolution in American tradition; but it would be difficult to say whether they added anything of an enduring nature to that tradition.[16]

Then there were the chroniclers, with those wonderfully Biblical names: Abiel Holmes, Hezekiah Niles, and Jedidiah Morse. Their documentary compilations were barely arranged in any logical order, despite this delightful assertion by Holmes in the preface to his 1829 edition:

> Without [chronological] arrangement, effects would often be placed before causes; contemporary characters and events disjoined; actions, having no relation to each other, confounded; and much of the pleasure and benefit, which History ought to impart, would be lost. If history, however, without chronology, is dark and confused; chronology, without history, is dry and insipid.[17]

What is most interesting about the 1820s, perhaps, is that many Americans in various ways became engaged in a quest for political order, social stability, and national identity. The last survivors of the Revolution were now cherished—their memories and, to a lesser degree, their guidance, were sought. Daniel Webster made a lengthy visit to Monticello in 1824, for example, and had extensive conversations with Jefferson, who reminisced at length about the Revolution. As Webster wrote subsequently to a friend:

> Mr. Jefferson is full of conversation, & as it relates, pretty much, to by-gone times, it is replete with information & useful anecdote. All

[16] See William R. Smith, *History as Argument: Three Patriot Historians of the American Revolution* (The Hague: Mouton, 1966); and Arthur H. Shaffer, *The Politics of History: Writing the History of the American Revolution, 1783–1815* (Chicago: Precedent, 1975).

[17] Abiel Holmes, *The Annals of America* (Cambridge, Mass.: Hilliard and Brown, 1829), vol. 1, Preface, p. 1. See also Hezekiah Niles, *Principles and Acts of the Revolution in America* (Baltimore: W. D. Niles, 1822); Jedidiah Morse, *Annals of the American Revolution* (Hartford, 1824).

the great men of our Revolutionary epoch necessarily had a circle of which they were, severally, the centre. Each, therefore, has something to tell not common to all. Mr. [John] Adams & Mr. Jefferson, for example, tho' acting together, on a common theatre, at Philadelphia, were nevertheless far apart, when in Massachusetts & Virginia, & each was at home, in the midst of men, & of events, more or less different from those which surrounded the other.[18]

Jared Sparks first appeared on the scene and played an interesting role, serving as chaplain in the House of Representatives from 1821 to 1823. He met and gathered information from many persons who had known George Washington and his political circle. Sparks thereby added to the stock of revolutionary lore accumulating in oral tradition and, equally important perhaps, became fired with enthusiasm for his life's work. "I have got a passion for revolutionary history," Sparks wrote in 1826, "and the more I look into it the more I am convinced that no complete history of the American Revolution has been written." [19]

Sparks, a New Englander, made an extraordinary research trip through the southern states in 1826, gathering up or copying documents in public repositories and private hands. By 1828 he was receiving reports on the Revolution and letters of interpretation from elder statesmen, such as this one from James Madison in January of that year:

It has always been my impression that a reestablishment of the colonial relations to the parent country previous to the controversy was the real object of every class of the people, till despair of obtaining it, and the exasperating effects of the war, and the manner of conduct-

---

[18] See *The Papers of Daniel Webster: Correspondence*, ed. Charles M. Wiltse (Hanover, N.H.: University Press of New England, 1974), vol. 1, p. 381. A conceptual framework for the tentative role of tradition in the 1820s, as well as some interesting comparisons, emerge from a contextual reading of two essays by Clifford Geertz, "Ideology as a Cultural System," and "After the Revolution: The Fate of Nationalism in the New States," in Geertz, *The Interpretation of Cultures: Selected Essays* (New York: Basic Books, 1973), pp. 183–254.

[19] Jared Sparks to Alexander Everett, Sept. 12, 1826, in *The Life and Writings of Jared Sparks*, ed. Herbert Baxter Adams (Boston: Houghton, Mifflin, 1893), vol. 1, p. 509. See also Sparks, "Materials for American History," *North American Review*, 23 (Oct., 1826): 275–294.

ing it, prepared the minds of all for the event declared on the 4th of July, 1776. . . .[20]

I find it very revealing, and symptomatic of a powerful tendency at work by the later 1820s, that Madison's stress should be so strongly upon the cautious *reluctance* of the revolutionaries. It contrasts markedly with his emphasis 40 years before, when he proudly praised the founders for their bold vision and deliberate innovation. "They accomplished a Revolution which has no parallel in the annals of human society," he wrote in 1787. "They reared the fabrics of governments [the state constitutions of 1776–1780] which have no model on the face of the globe." [21]

Sparks began to work on his huge George Washington editorial project in 1827. It occupied him for a decade and eventually resulted between 1834 and 1837 in the publication of 12 volumes of letters. During this period, Sparks also edited the *Diplomatic Correspondence of the American Revolution* (1829–1830) in 12 volumes, and *The Works of Benjamin Franklin* (1836–1840) in 10. Indeed, Sparks began to have a rather proprietary feeling about his role as *the* editor and historian of our Revolution. In 1833, when he learned that Edward Everett planned an edition of Franklin's papers, Sparks determined to beat Everett with his own set of Franklin's letters. In 1840, Sparks became very upset by the prospect that his general history of the Revolution—always envisioned but never written—would be pre-empted by George Bancroft. Sparks pleaded with William Hickling Prescott to divert Bancroft by enticing him to write a biography of Philip II of Spain, but to no avail.

Before considering the 1840s, this question must be answered: Why is 1832 a crucial year in this conjectural chronology? There are several reasons. First, the centennial of George Washington's birth, celebrated in 1832, seemed to denote a certain historical distance from the world of the founders. The centennial was marred, moreover, by a quarrelsome, petty divisiveness which

[20] James Madison to Jared Sparks, January 25, 1828, in Adams, *Life and Writings of Jared Sparks*, vol. 2, p. 219.
[21] *The Federalist Papers*, ed. Clinton Rossiter (New York: New American Library, 1961), p. 104.

contrasted with the comparative consensus of 1826, the fiftieth anniversary of the Declaration of Independence. In 1832, for instance, a great controversy arose over whether to dig up Washington's remains from his tomb at Mount Vernon and rebury him beneath the rotunda of the Capitol. Among all the arguments and counter-arguments, my favorite came from Wiley Thompson, a congressman from Georgia:

> In the march of improvement, and the rapid progress of the increase of population in the United States, it is probable that our settlements will not only extend to the Rocky Mountains, but reach beyond, stretching down to the Pacific coast. But say that the foot of the Rocky Mountains will form their western boundary—and we may reasonably suppose that this will happen at no distant period—then bring the great, the powerful West to act upon a proposition to remove the site of the Federal Government, and who can doubt that a location more central will be found and established on the banks of the Ohio? Shall the remains of our Washington be left amidst the ruins of this capitol, surrounded by the desolation of this city?

To this, Joel B. Sutherland of Pennsylvania retorted: "If our population is to reach to the Western Ocean, and the seat of Government to be removed, when we carry away the ensigns of power from this place, we will carry with us the sacred bones of Washington." [22]

The second reason why 1832 marks a watershed in the American sense of tradition, and perhaps a more important one, is that Charles Carroll died that year—the last surviving signer of the Declaration of Independence. As the *Daily National Intelligencer* put it, Americans were "feelingly alive to the privation sustained by the Republic, in the death of the last of her fathers." Contemporaries sensed the end of an era. [23]

[22] Charles Warren, "How Politics Intruded into the Washington Centenary of 1832," *Proceedings of the Massachusetts Historical Society*, 65 (1932):45–46; compare Warren's treatment of 1832 with Lyman H. Butterfield, "The Jubilee of Independence, July 4, 1826," *Virginia Magazine of History and Biography*, 61 (1953): 119–140.

[23] See Robert P. Hay, "Charles Carroll and the Passing of the Revolutionary Generation," *Maryland Historical Magazine*, 67 (1972): 54–62 and "The Glorious Departure of the American Patriarchs," *Journal of Southern History*, 35 (1969): 543–555.

III. The Revolution Recorded, Threatened, and Vindicated, 1833–1874

During this third, and in many respects most critical phase, intergenerational perceptions and anxieties affected the revolutionary tradition in fundamental ways. In 1836, the Democratic Party in New York urged upon the electorate the need "from time to time to resurvey the political ground which we have occupied; to look up ancient monuments, and see whether we are within the pale of our original faith." In 1840 an anonymous polemicist cited, with invidious comparison to the present, the "stern courage of our revolutionary sires." And the most constant refrain of these decades, repeatedly invoked with reference to the revolutionary tradition, was this one:

Fathers! have ye bled in vain?

It recurs over and over again in odes and orations of the 1830s, 1840s, and 1850s, in the South as well as in the North. It raises explicitly the questions that seem to have been on so many minds: Are we worthy of our revolutionary forebears? Are we undoing, by our divisiveness, all that they worked so hard to achieve? [24]

Those founders whose longevity made them mentors to the Jacksonian generation helped to raise the level of anxiety. Jefferson, for instance, wrote to John Holmes, a senator from Maine, that

> I regret that I am now to die in the belief, that the useless sacrifice of themselves by the generation of 1776, to acquire self-government and happiness to their country, is to be thrown away by the unwise and unworthy passions of their sons, and that my only consolation is to be, that I live not to weep over it.[25]

[24] See Welter, *Mind of America*, p. 9; Paul C. Nagel, *One Nation Indivisible*, pp. 128–167 and *This Sacred Trust: American Nationality, 1798–1898* (New York: Oxford University Press, 1971) , pp. 109, 118.

[25] Jefferson to John Holmes, April 22, 1820, *The Works of Thomas Jefferson*, ed. Paul Leicester Ford (New York: G. P. Putnam's Sons, 1904–1905) , vol. 12, p. 159. For an insightful discussion of this period, see George B. Forgie, "Father Past and Child Nation: The Romantic Imagination and the Origins of the American Civil War" (Ph.D. dissertation, Stanford University, 1971) .

Many of the revolutionary sons felt this psychic pressure intensely and tried to fulfill their sense of responsibility by writing and editing books about the founders, most especially during the two decades following 1832. Hence William Jay's two-volume *Life of John Jay* (1833), or John Church Hamilton's two-volume *Life of Hamilton* (1834–1841), or Charles Francis Adams' two-volume *Letters of John Adams to His Wife* (1841), or Henry C. Van Schaack's *Life of Peter Van Schaack* (1842), or William B. Reed's two-volume *Life and Correspondence of Joseph Reed* (1847).

Their motives were clearly stated. First, as William Jay put it in his preface, there was the imperative of filial obligation: "The generation by whom the independence of these United States was established and secured, is rapidly passing away; and before long, we shall seek in vain for a patriot of the Revolution to receive our homage." Second, as Henry Van Schaack wrote, there was the straightforward urge to preserve precious information: "It seemed probable that the manuscripts and information in [Peter Van Schaack's] possession would be lost to the public unless submitted by himself."

One symptomatic consequence of these acts of filial obligation was an inversion in the pattern of book dedications. In 1817, William Wirt dedicated his *Patrick Henry* "to the young men of Virginia," and in 1822 Hezekiah Niles' *Principles and Acts of the Revolution* was "dedicated to the young men of the United States." In 1837, however, when Peter Force began to publish his *American Archives*—revolutionary source materials in a series of staggering proportions—his dedication was to the founding fathers. Others in this third period followed his example.

As the sectional crisis deepened, especially between the mid-1850s and the later 1860s, poignant lamentations and a sense of political inadequacy punctuated the sentences of those seeking to cope with national disunion and hoping to know where they had gone astray. In 1855, the *North American Review* ran an essay–review of three volumes of Bancroft's *History*. Its opening paragraph is revealing. "One by one they totter and die," it said, "the remnants of that sturdy race in whose ears the drums yet beat, in whose eyes the colors stream, as they tell to the children of their children the story of the Revolution, of its battles and its trials. It becomes us to save what is fading from the memory of men." Then, on the next page, came pangs of anxiety at their unworthiness, being lesser folk: "Filial duty and scholarly research bring every day to light more and more of their inmost thoughts, and we may well ask ourselves, why the cheek tingles when we think how pure they were, how few were their faults and frailties. . . . Those who fought the great battle,—better, alas! than we could fight it!" [26]

As late as 1868, politicians continued to sing variations on this theme, both because they believed in it and because it seemed to be so resonant in the national chambers of memory and self-doubt. Here is Samuel Tilden, for example, in a major address of 1868:

> Fellow-citizens, I can imagine that from the ethereal heights the men that made this government—your Washingtons, your Jeffersons, your Madisons—look down to see whether this generation is to fail in transmitting to their descendants the priceless inheritance of constitutional government. Washington himself—his tall and peerless form leans over from the midst of those patriots and statesmen of the Revolution, to see today what we are about to do. Shall we prove ourselves worthy of our ancestry? If so, then there will be hope, not only for this country, but also for the oppressed and down-trodden in every clime and in every age.[27]

Fulfilling the founders' expectations and preserving their achievements was the most persistent theme in the decades after 1832; yet it was by no means the only one in our revolutionary tradition at that time. In a more positive emphasis, the Revolution came to be regarded as a major point of demarcation in the history of mankind. Robert Rantoul, Jr., a Democratic reformer from Massachusetts, put it this way in a speech at Gloucester in 1833: "The independence of the United States of America is not only a marked epoch in the course of time, but it is indeed the end from which the new order of things is to be reckoned. It is the dividing

[26] "The Causes of the American Revolution," *North American Review*, 80 (April 1855) : 389–390.

[27] *The Writings and Speeches of Samuel J. Tilden*, ed. John Bigelow (New York: Harper, 1885) , vol. 1, pp. 451–452.

point in the history of mankind; it is the moment of the political regeneration of the world." By 1850, the revolutionary tradition was also being used in a very conservative fashion: to resist changes, either institutional or intellectual. One handy way to express opposition to any innovation was to argue that it was simply inconsistent with the principles of 1776 or 1787.[28]

These attitudes, responses, and uses of the Revolution were not the singular possession of any particular section, class, or social group. They were pervasive. Half a dozen individuals, however, were most instrumental in shaping America's sense of the spirit of 1776 during the middle third of the nineteenth century. I have already mentioned two of them: Jared Sparks, whose *Life of Washington* (1839) became a best seller and who prepared the first academic offering in an American college on the Revolution —a course of 12 lectures at Harvard, also in 1839; and Peter Force, the indefatigable editor who gathered together his vast (but never finished) *American Archives* with the help of a handsome congressional subsidy. When Force's volumes began to appear in 1838, one enthusiastic reviewer even placed a *curse* upon anyone who might say or do anything unfavorable about the project. To the best of my knowledge, this curse is unique in the annals of American historical reviewing!

> Before this, nine lives at least were necessary to gather together the materials of history; here are the clay, and the straw, every thing necessary but the forming hand; here are the sand and the ashes, and all that is needed for the pure crystal, save only the creative fire which is to fuse the base materials into beauty, transparency, and harmony. If any should undertake to stop the gathering together of these memorials of the revolution, may their minds be haunted by the hobgoblins of imperfect conceptions; may their midnight slumbers be disturbed by the ghosts of the heroes of '76, clamoring for just honors to glorious deeds; and when they come to die, may oblivion hide their shame, and their names perish from among men.[29]

[28] See Welter, *Mind of America*, pp. 4–5, 11–12.

[29] *North American Review*, 46 (April, 1838): 486. For Peter Force's political support and subsidy, see George H. Callcott, *History in the United States, 1800–1860* (Baltimore: Johns Hopkins Press, 1970), pp. 50–51. Oh that the Congress would be so generous in support of historical scholarship today!

The other four principals who preserved and enhanced the revolutionary tradition at this time were Benson J. Lossing, William Gilmore Simms, Lorenzo Sabine, and George Bancroft. Lossing's *Pictorial Field Book of the Revolution,* first serialized and then published in two stout volumes (1850, 1852), may have done more than any other publication to foster popular pride in the history of the United States during the second half of the nineteenth century. His interviews with octogenarian survivors of the War for Independence and his hundreds of woodcuts of revolutionary scenes and battle sites made the birth of a nation both palpable and visual at exactly the time when memories were growing dim, settlers were moving westward (more remote from erstwhile colonial localities), and new immigrants had no personal ties to the cosmic events of 1765–1789.[30]

Simms was important for his cycle of seven novels about the Revolution in the South (1836–1856); biographies like his *Life of Francis Marion,* a best seller in 1844; and such patriotic poems as "The Swamp Fox" and "Battle of Eutaw Springs."

Lorenzo Sabine, a Massachusetts man who lived in Maine near the Canadian border for many years (1821–1849), came to know the Tories and their descendants intimately. His *American Loyalists* (1847) remains a valuable, pioneering work; but it also stirred a heated controversy that would continue intermittently for decades thereafter—tangling up retrospective views of the Revolution with the bitterness of sectional strife. Sabine claimed that there had been fewer loyalists in New England than in the South, and he condemned South Carolina in particular as a hotbed of Toryism. "It is hardly an exaggeration," he wrote, "to add that more Whigs of New England were sent to [South Carolina's] aid, and now lie buried in her soil, then she sent from it to every scene of strife from Lexington to Yorktown." [31]

[30] See Alexander Davidson, "How Benson J. Lossing Wrote His Field Books of the Revolution," *The Papers of the Bibliographical Society of America,* 32 (1938): 57–64; David D. Van Tassel, "Benson J. Lossing: Pen and Pencil Historian," *American Quarterly* 6 (1954): 32–44; John T. Cunningham, "Historian on the Double," *American Heritage,* 19 (June, 1968): 55–64, 78–81.

[31] See David D. Van Tassel, *Recording America's Past: An Interpretation of the Development of Historical Studies in America, 1607–1884* (Chicago: University of Chicago Press, 1960), pp. 136–137. Sabine brought out a second, enlarged edition

Needless to say, William Gilmore Simms, a South Carolinian, could not allow that barb to go unanswered; and so the feud began. It raged for decades. Back in 1824, Daniel Webster had been generous in his praise of cooperation between New England and the South: "indeed *they made* the Revolution," he wrote.[32] By the early 1850s, that illusion of unity had gone aglimmering. Theodore Parker's sketches of *Historic Americans,* such as Franklin, Washington, Jefferson, and Adams, were clearly shaped by Parker's role in the antislavery campaign. First delivered as public lectures in 1858, it is significant that they were not published as a book until 1870.

George Bancroft's four volumes on the Revolution appeared between 1858 and 1874, years when the United States was distracted by national disunion, and perhaps least interested of any time in our entire history in the events surrounding 1776. Nevertheless, Bancroft remained both popular and influential, in part, I suspect, because he managed to be all things to all people. He argued, for instance, that the Revolution "was most radical in its character, yet achieved with such benign tranquility that even conservatism hesitated to censure." [33]

By 1874, however, when the last of Bancroft's volumes on the Revolution appeared, a new phase had begun to emerge—one which started by being remarkably *un*historical in its orientation, but ended (with the century) in maudlin nostalgia for tradition and some strange perversions of the past, as well.

IV. Celebrating the Present and Escaping into the Past, 1875–1906

Our Centennial activities and outlook involved not so much an assessment of the past as a celebration of the present accom-

---

in 1864, *Biographical Sketches of Loyalists of the American Revolution* (Boston: Little, Brown, 1864).

32 *Papers of Daniel Webster: Correspondence,* vol. 1, p. 373. See also John Hope Franklin, "The North, the South, and the American Revolution," *Journal of American History,* 62 (1975–76): 5–23.

33 George Bancroft, *History of the United States of America* (New York: D. Appleton, 1883), vol. 2, p. 326.

panied by high hopes for the future. The national mood in 1876 was ebullient, full of self-congratulation for a century of progress. Huge ceramic urns, made for the United States by the Haviland Company at Limoges, France, were emblazoned, respectively, "1777, THE STRUGGLE" and "1876 PROSPERITY." In Ithaca, New York, a massive banner stretched across State Street with these legends: "1776, LIBERTY" and "1876 REFORM."

There were a few doubts and doubters, to be sure. On July 1, 1876, for instance, an editorial appeared in the *Newark Daily Advertiser* which looked back searchingly to the jubilee year and concluded that in 1826 "patriotism was more fervent than at the present time. People lived a little closer to the fountain-head of liberty than we do now, and they had not fallen into the whirlpool of fast living which keeps the present generation on such a constant tensile strain." There was some concern and ambivalence about the moral consequences of material progress; yet the nation had finally started to recover from a serious depression, and most eyes looked ahead rather than backward in 1876. Here is a characteristic song of that year, taken from a *Centennial Songster:*

"UNCLE SAM'S A HUNDRED!"
Oh, ye Powers! what a roar.
Such was never heard before—
Thundering from shore to shore:
"Uncle Sam's a hundred!"

Cannons boom and trumpets bray,
Fiddles squeak and fountains play—
'Tis his great Centennial day—
"Uncle Sam's a hundred!"

Stalwart men and puny boys,
Maids and matrons swell the noise,
Every baby lifts its voice:
"Uncle Sam's a hundred!"

Nervous folks who dote on quiet,
Though they're half distracted by it,
Can't help mixing in the riot:
"Uncle Sam's a hundred!"

Brutes that walk and birds that fly,
On the earth or in the sky,
Join the universal cry:
"Uncle Sam's a hundred!"

By the late 1800s, however, several distinct developments had emerged which would permanently affect the revolutionary tradition in American thought. First, the decline of "romantic," narrative history—the history of Bancroft and Parkman—was accompanied by the rise of positivistic, "scientific" history—the history of John William Draper and Henry Adams, with its characteristic emphasis upon material advances and technological change. The locomotive had replaced the Conestoga wagon, for example, as our national beast of burden—a long-range transformation that seemed almost as significant as our political alteration of 1776 and constitutional evolution of 1787.

Second, although American historical writing became more nationalistic than ever, it also became much less national in scope. Instead, the last decades of the nineteenth century were characterized by a growing interest in regional and local history, especially the contributions made by particular localities to the revolutionary cause. These were years of active productivity for such historians of New England as Justin Winsor, John Gorham Palfrey, and Mellen Chamberlain.[34]

Third, it was a period when biographies of the founders became almost as popular as they had been in the first decades of the nineteenth century; but with one crucial difference. These latter-day biographies of Sam Adams, George Mason, Washington, Franklin, and the rest, usually took pains to deemphasize any radical activities or tendencies. Instead, the founders appeared as statesmen rather than politicians, nation builders rather than revolutionaries. It was a conservative era, and our revolutionaries were derevolutionized accordingly.[35]

Fourth, it was a period when the Revolution fully entered the mainstream of American literary history: partly because of major academic projects by Moses Coit Tyler of Cornell and

34 See Merrill Jensen, "Historians and the Nature of the American Revolution," in Ray A. Billington, ed., *The Reinterpretation of Early American History: Essays in Honor of John Edwin Pomfret* (New York: W. W. Norton, 1968), p. 118; Bernard Bailyn, "The Losers: Notes on the Historiography of Loyalism," an appendix in *The Ordeal of Thomas Hutchinson* (Cambridge: Harvard University Press, 1974), pp. 383–408; and Henry W. Haynes, "Memoir of Mellen Chamberlain," *Proceedings of the Massachusetts Historical Society*, 20 (1906–7): 119–146.

35 See Pauline Maier, "Coming to Terms with Samuel Adams," *American Historical Review*, 81 (1976): 15; Craven, *Legend of the Founding Fathers*, pp. 171–172.

Barrett Wendell of Harvard,[36] and partly because of the obsession with revolutionary America in juvenile fiction of the decades 1886 to 1906. Everett Tomlinson and James Otis Kaler are no longer household words in this country; but several generations of Americans grew up on books like *Washington's Young Aids* and *The Boys of Old Monmouth* by Tomlinson, or *Boston Boys of 1775* and *The Minute Boys of New York City* by Kaler.[37]

People made pilgrimages in those years to battle sites and other shrines of the Revolution, then published their accounts of these patriotic adventures in books which began in this manner: " 'What a spot this is, boys and girls!' Uncle Tom Dunlap exclaimed, with an impressive sweep of the hand. 'The atmosphere is fairly charged with patriotism; the air throbs with memories.' "[38]

And finally, to cap it all, the very last years of phase IV witnessed an obsession with transplanting revolutionary heroes to more suitable graves than their original burials had been able to provide. In 1905 John Paul Jones was dug up at the Protestant cemetery outside Paris, and eventually reburied at the Naval Academy in Annapolis. In 1909 Pierre L'Enfant was removed from the Digges family plot in Prince Georges County, Maryland, and reinterred at Arlington National Cemetery. Other examples might be cited; but the net effect should be clear. By the early 1900s, the American Revolution in national tradition had been trivialized—and to a large degree, derevolutionized.[39]

[36] Moses Coit Tyler, *The Literary History of the American Revolution, 1763–1783* (New York: G. P. Putnam's Sons, 1897); Barrett Wendell, *A Literary History of America* (New York: Charles Scribner's Sons, 1900).

[37] See Whitfield J. Bell, Jr., "Everett T. Tomlinson: New Jersey Novelist of the American Revolution," in William C. Wright, ed., *New Jersey in the American Revolution—Political and Social Conflict* (Trenton: New Jersey Historical Commission, 1974), pp. 76–88.

[38] Elbridge S. Brooks, *The Century Book of the American Revolution: The Story of the Pilgrimage of a Party of Young People to the Battlefields of the American Revolution* (New York: Century, 1897). See also Ernest C. Peixotto, *A Revolutionary Pilgrimage* (New York: Charles Scribner's Sons, 1917).

[39] See Richard Pritchett, "The Day the Liberty Bell Came to Boston" [June 17, 1903], *Yankee* (June, 1976): 79–81, 150–153.

V. Dull Scholars, Cynical Debunkers, and Patriots All, 1907–1944

The most curious feature of this next phase is that the United States moved from confident nationalism to cynical disillusionment following World War I, but then shifted slowly back to ardent patriotism based upon a reaffirmation of democracy.

At the very beginning of our century, the dominant voice in writing about the Revolution belonged to a Philadelphia lawyer and amateur scholar who did not even start to write colonial history until the age of 40. Then Sydney George Fisher (1856–1927) became determined to strip away the nonsense and nostalgia attributed to American origins by nineteenth-century writers. So he produced a steady flow of books and essays which gathered momentum in a revisionist direction. *The True Benjamin Franklin* (1899) sought to remove the myths and humanize Poor Richard. *The True History of the American Revolution* (1903) was overtly hostile toward George Bancroft, Richard Hildreth, and John Fiske. *The Struggle for American Independence* (1908), Fisher's major work, took two volumes to insist upon the inadequacy of all previous books on the Revolution. And in 1912 he presented to the American Philosophical Society a major paper concerning "The Legendary and Myth-making Process in Histories of the American Revolution." [40]

In retrospect, however, Fisher seems significant not as the progenitor of a new approach or interpretation of the Revolution, but rather as the last gasp of a dying breed. From David Ramsay until Sydney George Fisher, serious scholarship had not been incompatible with popular appeal to a broad readership. Ramsay and Sparks, Bancroft and Lossing, Winsor and Fisher all worked close to the primary materials. Their analyses may sometimes seem naïve or even misguided today; but they made a genuine effort

[40] Sydney George Fisher, "The Legendary and Myth-Making Process in Histories of the American Revolution," *Proceedings of the American Philosophical Society*, 51 (April, 1912): 53–75. See also Lawrence H. Gipson, *The British Empire Before the American Revolution*, 15 vols. (New York: Alfred A. Knopf, 1936–1970), vol. 13, pp. 363–367.

to ground their writings deeply in the sources. Nevertheless, they also had a very wide appeal to laymen and enjoyed large sales.

After about 1910, however, "scholars" and "popularizers" began to appear as separate categories. The latter wrote well but depended upon superficial information. The former probed our revolutionary roots more deeply than ever before, but their writings were more narrowly monographic, their prose commonly mediocre; and their audiences shrank accordingly. Claude Van Tyne, George Louis Beer, Carl Becker, Charles McLean Andrews, Arthur Schlesinger, Sr., Charles McIlwain, and J. Franklin Jameson all had very important new insights concerning the Revolution. Between 1905 and 1931 they poured out volumes of first-class history; yet their appeal lay almost entirely *within* the academy, their influence upon national tradition was minimal. Only Becker (at times) and Charles A. Beard seemed able to bridge that growing gap between the respectable and the readable; and Beard's legacy in writing about the Revolution may have been primarily to pave the way for those heady debunkers of the 1920s.

And how they debunked! D. H. Lawrence brought out his *Studies in Classic American Literature* in 1922, William Carlos Williams his *In the American Grain* in 1925. William E. Woodward published *George Washington—the Image and the Man* in 1926, and Rupert Hughes his *George Washington—the Human Being and the Hero* between 1926 and 1930 in three volumes. Along with many of their contemporaries, they produced iconoclastic books which titillated by knocking erstwhile idols off their pedestals. Still others, meanwhile, began to reconsider the very essence of democratic theory; and when they found it wanting, as Ezra Pound did, decided to use the revolutionary era as a medium for their ire. The "New Hamiltonians," as Merrill Peterson has called them, had a big time of it during these years.[41]

By the mid-1930s, however, Jefferson's stock was rising while Hamilton's was declining. Carl Van Doren could resuscitate Frank-

[41] See Merrill Peterson, *The Jefferson Image in the American Mind* (New York: Oxford University Press, 1962), pp. 333–347; Frederick Sanders, *John Adams Speaking: Pound's Sources for the Adams Cantos* (Orono: University of Maine, 1975); and Edward A. Purcell, Jr., *The Crisis of Democratic Theory* (Lexington: University Press of Kentucky, 1973).

lin as the self-made exemplar of a democratic society;[42] and Esther Forbes selected an artisan of humble origins around whom to spin her charming story of American Independence: *Paul Revere and the World He Lived In* (1942). There's nothing quite like the threat of totalitarianism to make us reaffirm democracy. Imperfect though democracy may be, we have yet to find a superior system; and by the early 1940s its roots in our revolutionary heritage received considerable emphasis from born-again patriots.

VI. Realism, Pluralism, and Elitism: The Revolutionary Tradition Recedes, 1945–1975

In looking at the literature of the last 30 years, I am most impressed by a pervasive stress upon the positive role of elites, charismatic leadership, and realism about human nature in revolutionary America. The democratic dogmas of World War II now seemed foolishly innocent. Starry-eyed optimism was replaced by wide-eyed cynicism. Consequently there would be much greater emphasis upon the constructive nation making of 1787 than upon the destructive break with Britain in 1776.

Among the popular writers, there appeared a pronounced shift to the right. Howard Fast broke with the Communist Party during the 1950s. Although he continued to write novels about the Revolution, his former Marxist edge was gone. His human sympathies remained strong, to be sure, but *April Morning* (1961) and *The Hessian* (1971) are more nearly psychological novels than didactic dramas of class conflict and exploitation.[43]

John Dos Passos, whose leftist sympathies had remained

---

[42] Carl Van Doren, *Benjamin Franklin* (New York: Viking Press, 1938), *Secret History of the American Revolution* (New York: Viking Press, 1941), *Mutiny in January* (New York: Viking Press, 1943); Van Doren, ed., *Benjamin Franklin's Autobiographical Writings* (New York: Viking Press, 1945).

[43] For his break with the Soviet Union, see Howard Fast, *The Naked God: The Writer and the Communist Party* (New York: Praeger, 1957), pp. 194–197; and John P. Diggins, *Up from Communism: Conservative Odysseys in American Intellectual History* (New York: Harper and Row, 1975), p. 433.

strong throughout the 1930s and World War II, thereafter found a new meaning for freedom in Jeffersonian individualism. In a series of nonfiction works published between 1954 and 1966, Dos Passos quite candidly admired the founding fathers for their capacity as a ruling elite. John Diggins has recently observed that Dos Passos discovered in the founders "legitimate moral authority that could be entrusted with power." [44]

Others were equally fascinated by the quality of leadership an elite could produce. Hence, Douglas Southall Freeman's massive *Washington* (1948–1957) in seven volumes, and James Flexner's more modest *Washington* (1965–1972) in four; or Catherine Drinker Bowen's *John Adams and the American Revolution* (1950). Theorists of revolution, meanwhile, could find little that was truly revolutionary in our achievement of independence. "Even if one resists this temptation to equate revolution with the struggle for liberation," wrote Hannah Arendt, "instead of identifying revolution with the foundation of freedom, there remains the additional, and in our context more serious, difficulty that there is very little in form or content of the new revolutionary constitutions which was even new, let alone revolutionary." [45]

Within the academy, meanwhile, a subtle kind of shift occurred. To call it a "conservative" shift would be misleading; for the word has too many inappropriate connotations, and many of the professional historians involved were themselves political liberals on matters of reform, race, McCarthyism, and the Great Society programs. They arrived at their conclusions, moreover, by different routes and for varied reasons. Nonetheless, the net effect after several decades was to minimize the radicalism and innovations of 1776. As William Nelson wrote in 1965: "In reading much of the current literature on the Revolution, one has sometimes the

---

[44] Diggins, *Up from Communism*, pp. 95–96 and "Visions of Chaos and Visions of Order: Dos Passos as Historian," *American Literature*, 46 (November, 1974): 329–346. See John Dos Passos, *The Head and Heart of Thomas Jefferson* (Garden City: Doubleday, 1954), *The Men Who Made the Nation* (Garden City: Doubleday, 1957), *The Shackles of Power: Three Jeffersonian Decades* (Garden City: Doubleday, 1966).

[45] Hannah Arendt, *On Revolution* (New York: Viking Press, 1963), p. 141. On Arendt's anticommunist conservatism, see Diggins, *Up from Communism*, p. 430.

feeling that there is nothing missing from it except the Revolution itself." [46]

Leonard Labaree wrote with sympathy about the "Nature of American Loyalism" (1945); and Cecelia Kenyon praised the Founding Fathers for their realism as practical politicians (1951). She admired them for being more tough-minded than Tom Paine about the imperfections of democracy.[47] In *The Genius of American Politics* (1953), Daniel Boorstin did his best to depict the revolutionaries as cautious legalists; and Robert E. Brown's revisionist *Middle-Class Democracy and the Revolution in Massachusetts, 1691–1780* (1955) persuaded many scholars to believe that no "internal" revolution had been necessary—merely a formal separation from Great Britain.

Charles Sydnor and John Roche both praised the founding fathers for bringing to power a "democratic elite," while Martin Diamond admired them for being cautious and realistic about the pitfalls of democracy. He considered the Declaration of Independence a recklessly populistic document, devoid of guidance on the proper shape of democratic institutions:

> Our Founding Fathers more skeptically, sensibly, and soberly, were concerned how to make this new government *decent even though democratic*. All the American revolutionaries, whether they were partisans of the theory that democratic republics had to be small or agrarian or only loosely confederated in order to remain free, or whether they retained the traditional idea that democracy had to be counterbalanced by nobility or wealth, or whether they subscribed to

[46] William Nelson, "The Revolutionary Character of the American Revolution," *American Historical Review*, 70 (1965): 1002; cf. Marian J. Morton, *The Terrors of Ideological Politics: Liberal Historians in a Conservative Mood* (Cleveland: Press of Case Western Reserve University, 1972), especially Chapters 4 and 5; and for my own perspective upon the "schools" of Bernard Bailyn and Merrill Jensen, see Michael Kammen, "The American Revolution Bicentennial and the Writing of Local History," *History News*, 30 (August, 1975).

[47] Leonard Labaree, "The Nature of American Loyalism," *Proceedings of the American Antiquarian Society*, 54 (1945): 15–58; Cecelia Kenyon, "Where Paine Went Wrong," *American Political Science Review*, 65 (1951): 1086–1099. See also Adrienne Koch, *Power, Morals, and the Founding Fathers* (Ithaca: Cornell University Press, 1961), a book begun in 1952 and deeply affected by the attitudinal exigencies of the Cold War.

37

the large-republic theory implicit in the new Constitution—all the American revolutionaries knew that democracy was a problem in need of constant solution, in constant need of moderation, in constant need of institutions and measures to mitigate its defects and guard against its dangers.[48]

Finally, it is more than fortuitous that a founder hitherto neglected came to be recognized in these years as an intellectual giant. James Madison emerged after World War II as the most carefully studied of American theorists. A kind of cult figure on many campuses, he came to be seen as the most perceptive, original, and visionary among his peers. *Federalist* Number 10, I am sure, was more closely scrutinized in the 1950s and 1960s than either the Declaration of Independence or the Bill of Rights! Madison's sophisticated interest-group analysis, his realism about the nature of man as a political animal, and his profound understanding of the role of public opinion—all received lavish praise. Madison the modern pluralist, the student of governmental mechanisms, and the nationalist, had important messages for Americans during the three decades following 1945.[49]

Within each of my six periods, there is discernible movement and change—often a pronounced shift in attitudes—yet each phase

---

[48] Charles Sydnor, *American Revolutionaries in the Making: Political Practices in Washington's Virginia* (Chapel Hill: University of North Carolina Press, 1952) ; John Roche, "The Founding Fathers: A Reform Caucus in Action," *American Political Science Review* 55 (1961) : 799–816; Martin Diamond, "The Revolution of Sober Expectations," in *The American Revolution: Three Views* (New York: American Brands, Inc., 1975) , pp. 57–85. The quotation is from page 79.

[49] See Irving Brant, *James Madison*, 6 vols. (Indianapolis: Bobbs-Merrill, 1941–1961) , and *The Fourth President: A Life of James Madison* (Indianapolis: Bobbs-Merrill, 1970) ; Ralph Ketcham, *James Madison* (New York: Macmillan, 1971) ; Marvin Meyers, ed., *The Mind of the Founder: Sources of the Political Thought of James Madison* (Indianapolis: Bobbs-Merrill, 1973) ; Merrill D. Peterson, ed., *James Madison: A Biography in His Own Words* (New York: Harper and Row, 1974) ; Marvin Meyers, "Founding and Revolution: A Commentary on Publius-Madison," in Stanley Elkins and Eric McKitrick, eds., *The Hofstadter Aegis: A Memorial* (New York: Alfred A. Knopf, 1974) , pp. 3–35; Paul F. Bourke, "The Pluralist Reading of James Madison's Tenth Federalist," in *Perspectives in American History*, 9 (1975) : 271–295.

had a certain cohesion. The first (1776–1799) involved a search for the Revolution's proper meaning and implications. The second (1800–1832) saw the passing of the founders and thereby the end of oral verification. In the third (1833–1874) the Revolution came to be understood in the light of those issues which precipitated the Civil War; and despite a desire to fulfill the founders' goals in order to save the Revolution from oblivion, memories of it began to fade in the 1860s.[50] It is more than symbolic that the Washington Monument remained unfinished until 1885.

The fourth phase (1875–1906) began with a celebration of progress and the present, but ended in manipulation of the past as a dream world. When our own century opened, the Revolution had been derevolutionized. Between 1907 and 1944 we moved from nationalism to cynicism and then back to patriotism; so the Revolution's role in American tradition underwent adjustments accordingly. Since 1945 historians have tended to minimize the Declaration, maximize the achievements of that grand convention held at Philadelphia in 1787, and, most of all, emphasize the role of elites, interest groups, public opinion, and other political agencies whose importance was only implicitly recognized back in the eighteenth century.

During phase I, the Revolution's future place in American tradition was uncertain, and it remained ambivalent in phase II. By the late 1820s, however, the balance began to tip visibly toward a more conservative view. John Randolph expressed contempt for anyone who might perceive a resemblance between our own Revolution and those contemporary movements for independence in Latin America. When John Trumbull, the great artist–historian of the American Revolution, published his *Autobiography* in 1841, he remarked that

> The calm splendor of our own Revolution, comparatively rational and beneficial as it had been, was eclipsed in the meteoric glare and horrible blaze of glory of republican France; and we, who in our own case, had scarcely stained the sacred robe of rational liberty with a

50 See George Fitzhugh, "Revolutions of '76 and '61 Contrasted," *De Bow's Review*, 4 (July–August, 1867):36–47.

single drop of blood unnecessarily shed, learned to admire that hideous frenzy which made the very streets of Paris flow with blood.[51]

The balance had not been tipped entirely, however, nor irrevocably so. In 1851, Horatio Greenough, the sculptor, informed William Cullen Bryant (who had written many popular poems about the Revolution) that

> I wish to erect a monument which shall record on the same spot—the treason of Arnold—the capture and death of Andre and the fate of Capt'n Hale. I believe this idea may take a form exceedingly significant of our system, highly expressive of our democratic ethics—& a caution to egotistical intrigue.[52]

Yet the conservative view of our Revolution as being unique, comparatively bloodless, completed and fulfilled by 1789 grew steadily stronger during the second half of the nineteenth century. Although the Revolution remained central to our sense of nationality, *pari passu* it also became trivialized. Subtly, steadily, the American Revolution became a War for Independence and a backward-looking struggle simply to preserve the rights of Englishmen. The special virtue of our Minutemen, apparently, was that they respected Magna Charta and the Petition of Right more vigorously than George III or Lord North.

So the story stood in national tradition as late as 1975. In 1976 the pendulum of interpretation was beginning to swing back, at least partially. Current work being done by Gordon Wood, Eric Foner, and Alfred Young, to name just a few, suggests a new emphasis upon profound changes which began in 1776, as well as a radical legacy which endured beyond 1800, a legacy which Wood has called "The Democratization of Mind in the American Revolution."[53]

[51] See Butterfield, "The Jubilee of Independence," 132; *The Autobiography of Colonel John Trumbull, Patriot–Artist, 1756–1843*, ed. Theodore Sizer (New Haven: Yale University Press, 1953) , p. 172.

[52] Horatio Greenough to William Cullen Bryant, May 7, 1851, in *Letters of Horatio Greenough, American Sculptor*, ed. Nathalia Wright (Madison: University of Wisconsin Press, 1972) , p. 390.

[53] Gordon Wood's essay, part of a much larger book which he is writing, appears in *Leadership in the American Revolution: Papers Presented at the Third*

I also see signs that the sharp bifurcation of scholarly and popular perceptions may be diminishing somewhat, thanks to genuine cooperation between academe and the media in the presentation of such successful series as *The Adams Chronicles, Ourstory,* and *Suddenly an Eagle.*

It is much too early to say, however, whether these tendencies are more than ephemeral and whether they will outlive the special focus of 1976. There is, alas, a real likelihood that the Bicentennial year will leave a massive legacy of Bicentennial boredom. I hope not, for as Francis Calley Gray put it, in a Fourth of July oration given in 1818, "When the history of our ancestors is forgotten, there is your liberty destroyed."

Symposium, May 9 and 10, 1974 (Washington: Library of Congress, 1974), pp. 63–88. See also Eric Foner, *Tom Paine and Revolutionary America* (New York: Oxford University Press, 1976); Alfred F. Young, ed., *The American Revolution: Explorations in the History of American Radicalism* (DeKalb: Northern Illinois University Press, 1976) and "Interdisciplinary Studies of the American Revolution," a special issue of *The Journal of Interdisciplinary History* 6 (Spring, 1976), especially pp. 545–677. It is significant, too, that the 1976 Jefferson Lectures in the Humanities were given from coast to coast by John Hope Franklin on the subject of "Racial Equality in America," and that the most striking Bicentennial series on television was a 12-part adaptation of *Roots* (1976) by Alex Haley—a personalized rendition of Afro-American history.

II

THE PERSPECTIVE
OF CONFLICT

3

Collective Action
in England and America,
1765-1775
Charles Tilly

The Gentleman's Magazine and Historical Chronicle still makes lively reading 200 years later. The self-styled "Sylvanus Urban, Gent." edited the monthly from 1731 onward. His magazine carried a miscellany of essays, announcements, and news items, the last often clipped unceremoniously from other publications. It also contained a haphazard chronology of current events. In 1765, the presumably gentle readers of the monthly encountered many reports of protests and demands both from within England and from the rest of the British-dominated world. The British government faced a fiscal crisis because of the cost of the Seven Years' War, now 2 years ended. It was devising new taxes to pay its debts, including high levies on commercial transactions imposed by requiring the use of stamped paper.

To make things worse, food shortages were growing and prices rising, to the accompaniment of complaints from city and country alike. *Gentleman's Magazine,* January number, reported that on the tenth:

> Some thousands of weavers went in a body and presented the following petition to both houses of Parliament: *Lords and Gentlemen.* The humble petition of the journeyman silkweavers, on behalf of themselves, and great numbers of poor people in the same trade. *Sheweth:* That through the badness of trade, many hundreds of your humble petitioners are actually without work, others dread shortly to undergo the same fate. Our wives, sons and daughters, are mostly without employ, and consequently many of us are in the utmost poverty and want. It is these thoughts that throw us almost into despair, and induce us to throw ourselves at your feet, humbly begging your assistance in this our lamentable condition.

Lamentations over, they came to the specific supplication—that importation and sale of foreign silks be banned. Four days later, according to *Gentleman's Magazine:*

> A tumultuous mob assembled in the borough of *Devises,* and being armed and disguised, assaulted the houses of several of the principal inhabitants, particularly the mayor's, the under-sheriff's, and town-clerk's, the distributor of stamps, the post-master's tatler's, and the excise office, with divers others, and demolished the windows, destroyed the furniture, and threatened the lives of the occupiers.[1]

Whereas the "thousands of weavers" had marched through London streets in orderly fashion, the "tumultuous mob" of Devises thus took more direct action.

On the twenty-fourth there was more petitioning:

> At a court of aldermen at *Guildhall* a petition having been drawn up and agreed to be presented to the honourable House of Commons, on occasion of the hardships the poor labour under from the present dearness of bread, and the likelihood of its being much dearer, if the exportation of corn should continue, the sheriffs of this city went from Guildhall about twelve o'clock, and presented the said petition to that honourable house.[2]

Bread prices figured in many a news item during 1765. In February, prices rose enough to require cancellation of the usual bounty paid for grain exports, and in August provincial food riots persuaded Parliament to permit the importation of grain duty-free.

[1] *Gentleman's Magazine and Historical Chronicle* (London), 1765, p. 94.
[2] Ibid., p. 44.

Bread-and-butter issues, literally and figuratively, filled the British news columns for 1765.

Gentleman's Magazine gave ample attention to the North American military campaigns within the struggle the British later called the Seven Years' War and the Americans remembered as the French and Indian War. However, the magazine carried little domestic news from America before 1765. That year, in February, it reported that three Cherokee chiefs were presented to the Lords of Trade and Plantations; they complained of encroachment on their hunting grounds and requested the dispatch of "learned persons" to "instruct them in the knowledge of things." [3] Later in the year, the magazine began printing accounts of protests and demands in the American colonies rather frequently. The Stamp Act figured in most of them.

The Stamp Act of 1765 extended to America a tax already being collected in Britain. Proclaimed in March, the levy on publications and transactions was to take effect in November. Long before then, however, the resistance began. The October issue of *Gentleman's Magazine* carried an account of Boston's response to the arrival of the stamped paper in August. Part of it ran:

> A dangerous multitude had assembled some days before, and had demolished an edifice lately erected, as was supposed for a stamp office, attacked the court of the deputy register of the court of vice-admiralty, entered a dwelling-house of Mr. Hollowell, and destroyed the rich and valuable furniture; burnt his papers, and purloined his money; and then proceeded to the mansion-house of his honour the Lieutenant Governor, which in a few hours they reduced to a mere skeleton; all the furniture, plate, glasses, china, wearing apparel, his valuable and costly library, the files and records of office, fell a prey to their destructive rage.[4]

Gentleman's Magazine was describing the famous attack on Thomas Hutchinson's residence, on the twenty-sixth of August. From that point on, the magazine reported American crowd actions and solemn deliberations alike. By the end of November 1765, *Gentleman's Magazine* was commenting, "It is confidently

3 Ibid., p. 95.
4 Ibid., p. 474.

asserted, that if the new stamp act is ever carried into execution in that continent, it must be by military collectors; for no person in civil employ will dare to undertake it." [5] The prediction was accurate.

American historians know these events well. They are a traditional starting point for accounts of the colonial resistance to Britain which eventuated in the American Revolution a decade later. Yet it is worth examining them again, in the company of English conflicts during the same period.

That connection, too, has been made before. Many historians have noted that the American cause entered the debate over political rights with England, and attracted such eminent defenders as Edmund Burke. Pauline Maier and W. A. Smith have analyzed the parallels between the American remonstrances and the new popular movement for liberty of expression which grew up in England during the same decade around the sharp-tongued governmental critic, John Wilkes.[6] And a few American historians, stirred by George Rudé's studies of European crowds, have compared the actions of crowds in Europe and America.[7]

Yet the comparison has not worn itself out. For one thing, our knowledge of the forms, occasions, and meanings of crowd actions on both sides of the Atlantic has deepened considerably

[5] Ibid., p. 537.

[6] Pauline R. Maier, "Popular Uprisings and Civil Authority in Eighteenth-Century America," *William and Mary Quarterly*, 3rd ser., 27 (1970): 3–35; William Ander Smith, "Anglo-Colonial Society and the Mob, 1740–1775" (Ph.D. Dissertation, Claremont Graduate School and University Center, 1965). See, also, Lloyd I. Rudolph, "The Eighteenth-Century Mob in America and Europe," *American Quarterly*, 11 (1959): 447–469.

[7] George Rudé, *Wilkes and Liberty* (Oxford: Clarendon Press, 1962), *The Crowd in History* (New York: Wiley, 1964), and *Hanoverian London: 1714–1808* (London: Secker & Warburg, 1971). See, also, Dirk Hoerder, *Crowd Action in a Revolutionary Society: Massachusetts, 1765–1780* (New York: Academic Press, forthcoming). And in Alfred F. Young, ed., *The American Revolution: Explorations in the History of American Radicalism* (De Kalb: Northern Illinois University Press, 1976) see Edward Countryman, "'Out of the Bounds of the Law': Northern Land Rioters in the Eighteenth Century," pp. 37–69; Marvin L. Michael Kay, "The North Carolina Regulation, 1766–1776: A Class Conflict," pp. 71–123; Ronald Hoffman, "The 'Disaffected' in the Revolutionary South," pp. 273–316; and Alfred F. Young, "Afterword," pp. 447–462.

since Rudé's pioneering essays appeared. Increasingly we recognize the place of ritual, street theater, and exemplary punishment within the apparent chaos and bloodletting of eighteenth-century crowd actions; more and more we see how regularly the crowd's central action played out—sometimes mockingly, sometimes in dead seriousness—the role of the local authorities with respect to the problem at hand, such as in the trial of a malefactor, or the supervision of marketing.

For another thing, we are learning to put direct crowd action into the whole range of collective action—violent and nonviolent —by which people expressed their interests, grievances, and aspirations. We begin to see that the behavior which contemporary authorities and subsequent historians called "mob'" actions were simply the most concentrated and visible events in what were typically long series of efforts to express the same popular interests, grievances, and aspirations. Thus machine breaking occurred amid appeals to local authorities for prohibition of the offending machines, and forcible invasions of enclosed fields accompanied or followed community lawsuits to protect individual land use.

Both the highly visible and the obscure efforts, it turns out, generally took one or another of a few standardized forms varying from one group or time to another but quite characteristic of a particular group and time; each time and place has its own limited repertoire of collective actions; ordinary Anglo-Americans of the eighteenth century knew how to forward their interests by petitioning, by inflicting punishments such as tarring and feathering, and by acting through some kinds of local assemblies, but not generally by forming associations, conducting electoral campaigns, or organizing strikes in the nineteenth-century manner.

As the comparison of the eighteenth and nineteenth centuries suggests, the historical study of collective action has two faces: On the one side, the forms of action bear all the marks of particular cultures, everyday local life, accumulated traditions, and specific interests; on the other side, changes in the form, intensity, and locus of collective action record the great transformations of interests and social organization in the world at large. Over the Western world as a whole, to put it very schematically, the seven-

49

teenth century brought tax rebellions, the eighteenth century food riots, the nineteenth century strikes and demonstrations. And why? Again, schematically, because in the seventeenth century the salient challenge to ordinary peoples' interests was the recurrent fiscal pressure of expanding states, because in the eighteenth century the rapid growth of capitalism stepped up the demands of the national market on local food supplies as it increased the readiness of merchants and authorities to give priority to the national market, and because in the nineteenth century workers and bourgeois alike shifted their efforts away from defense of old local rights against the pressures of the state and capitalism toward attempts to acquire power over the new, large structures being created by capitalism and national states.[8] Thus the concrete local histories of collective action fit together into a general history of social change.

The evolution of collective action in eighteenth-century England and America also bears on two major subjects of historical debate—namely, the origins of the American Revolution and the outlines of a general revolutionary movement in Western culture near the end of the eighteenth century. The evolution of collective action after 1760 bears on the debate concerning the origins of the American Revolution because the comparison between England and America helps us decide whether Americans were already behaving as if they were distinct and independent by the time of the Stamp Act crisis, whether small clusters of influential people in various colonies maneuvered their particular class interests into a general definition of the colonies' interests, and whether a rapid *re*definition of the situation as revolutionary occurred in the colonies as 1776 approached. It bears on the debate concerning the so-called Atlantic Revolution because the comparison helps us determine whether ordinary people in both England and America moved toward a general demand for popular sovereignty and whether the American experience visibly influenced the English practice.

[8] Charles, Louise, and Richard Tilly, *The Rebellious Century: 1830–1930* (Cambridge: Harvard University Press, 1975).

Instead of taking on the full weight of these bulky questions, let us use a simple conceit to lighten the burden. Suppose we think of the American colonies that eventually formed the United States as just 13 more English counties—distant and little known to Londoners, perhaps, but still counties like Devon or Yorkshire. Suppressing the knowledge that those 13 counties would soon form an independent country, we can then ask how the news of collective action coming in from them during the 1760s and 1770s contrasted, if at all, with the news coming in from other English counties.

For further simplicity, let us focus on two rather different American colonies: Massachusetts and South Carolina. In the middle of the eighteenth century, Massachusetts combined the trading activity of Boston, then a city of 10,000 to 15,000 people, and a half-dozen other port cities of much smaller size with the farming of hundreds of other settlements spreading west. The English settlement in Massachusetts was already well over a century old. South Carolina was a newer colony, devoted largely to agriculture.

Neither Massachusetts nor South Carolina had anything like London. London was one of the world's great metropolises, a city of almost 700,000 people containing an imperial capital, housing a vast array of industry, trade, and services, and surrounded by a highly commercialized agricultural region. The comparison of London and England with Massachusetts and South Carolina is therefore nothing like a controlled experiment matching areas that resemble each other in all respects but one. Still the variety gives us a chance to ask whether the English and American areas each had something in common and whether similar processes of change were going on in all of them.

In a final simplification, let us emphasize two periods of time —1765–1766 and 1774–1775. Both were intervals of political turmoil on each side of the Atlantic, although for somewhat different reasons. At the start of 1765, the American colonies seemed more or less acquiescent in British rule, while England itself had just seen a serious challenge to its ruling class in the form of the first phase of the Wilkite movement. By the end of 1775, the American colonies were in rebellion, while the English at home seemed to have reached a characteristic compromise. Thus we know from the start that we have contrasting processes under examination.

I. Defense of Local Rights

In the England of 1765 and 1766, how did the ordinary people who shared an interest, grievance, or ambition act together, if and when they did? In those particular years, food riots were the most visible actions in England as a whole. As we have already noticed, high prices and shortages excited a few open conflicts in 1765. The next year brought the century's greatest stream of food riots. Seen close up, a food riot usually comprised one or a combination of four actions:

1. A tumultuous public gathering in which people demanded that the authorities act to bring down prices and increase the supply and threats against hoarders and profiteers were likely to be heard
2. A search of storehouses and private dwellings for hoarded grain and its forcible removal to public storage
3. The seizure and sale of food already on display, but at a publicly announced price significantly below the current market
4. The blockage and seizure of food being shipped through or from a locality

In 1766, attacks on local workhouses and flour mills also played a part in food riots. To quote from one of the many contemporary reports of September, 1766:

> A riotous mob assembled at Birmingham on the fair day there, and sold bread and cheese at their own prices; but being overpowered likewise by the civil magistrate's authority, their ringleaders were sent to gaol. At the same time an agreement was made with the bakers to make a sufficient quantity of household-bread, and to sell it at a penny a pound, by which means the people were pacified.
>
> At Nottingham fair the mob seized upon all the cheese the factors had purchased, and distributed the same among them, leaving the farmers

cheese unmolested. The military were called to the aid of the civil magistracy, but, luckily, one man only was killed, and that happened to be a farmer, a bystander.[9]

As these accounts suggest, most food riots were not violent in the sense of directly damaging persons or property; when people were hurt, it was ordinarily the militia or regular troops who hurt them. In that regard, the word "riot" is misleading. The essence of the action was to assert the local community's right to consume whatever food was available locally at a price the local poor could afford to pay and to demand that the authorities defend that right. Since in times of crisis the authorities had customarily commandeered the local food supply and arranged sales to the poor at prices they could afford, to some degree the so-called food riot simply called the authorities back to their customary duties or substituted the action of the crowd for the missing action of the authorities. The food riot defended the priority of the local community over the profits of merchants and over the demands of the national market.

The combination of defense of local rights and pressure on local authorities was a common feature of eighteenth-century popular collective action. One survey of riot accounts in *Gentleman's Magazine* and the *Annual Register* from 1740 to 1775 identifies 159 events.[10] Ninety-six were food riots, and 20 industrial disputes, while there were smaller numbers of actions against turnpike tolls, enclosures, conditions of military service, prisons, workhouses, and particular enemies of the local people. More than half the riots enumerated over the 36-year period, especially the food riots, occurred from 1765 through 1770. The important thing about the list is the reactive character of most of the events—that is, people were resisting threats to established rights in roads, common fields, local food supply, and so on, rather than demanding things they had never enjoyed. The broad theme of popular

9 *Annual Register* (London), 1765, p. 140. On British local conditions and turbulence, see John Bohstedt, "Riots in England, 1790–1810, with Special Reference to Devonshire" (Ph.D. dissertation, Harvard University, 1972); and David Jones, *Before Rebecca: Popular Protests in Wales, 1793–1835* (London: Allen Lane, 1973).

10 Smith, "Anglo-Colonial Society and the Mob," pp. 29–33.

collective action in eighteenth-century England was the defense of local rights against the rising pressure of capitalism.

II.   Events in London

If we shift our attention to London, however, we find different patterns of behavior. There, the most visible forms of popular collective action were aimed directly at major political figures and at Parliament. This does not mean it looked just like twentieth-century politics. On the fourteenth of February 1765, for example, a hackney coach brought bookseller John Williams to the pillory in New Palace Yard to receive his punishment for republishing John Wilkes' *North Briton*. Ten thousand people, reports the *Annual Register,* cheered him for the full hour he spent in the stocks:

> Opposite to the pillory were erected four ladders, with cords running from one ladder to another, on which were hung a jack boot, an axe, and a bonnet; the last with a label, Scotch bonnet; the boot and bonnet, after remaining there some time, were burnt, the tops of the boot having been previously chopped off. In the mean time a gentle·man, with a purple purse, ornamented with ribbons of an orange color, began a collection, in favour of Mr. Williams, by putting a guinea in himself; and then carrying it round, gave an opportunity to every one to contribute according to his fancy, by which means it is supposed Mr. Williams got above 200 guineas; one gentleman gave 50. Mr. Williams, at going into the pillory and getting out, bowed to the spectators; and held a sprig of laurel in his hand all the time. The same coach carried him back, and the master of it refused to take any hire.[11]

The boot and Scotch bonnet we will encounter again, in America; by pun and ethnic origin they identified the king's minister Lord Bute. The staging of the event was meticulous; it included the hiring of hackney coach number 45—the issue number of the *North Briton* for which Wilkes had originally been convicted.

Sometimes the same use of the city as a theater showed up in

---

[11] *Annual Register,* 1765, p. 65.

actions supporting the government. At the repeal of the American Stamp Act in 1766, for example,

> . . . the American merchants made a most numerous appearance, to express their gratitude and joy; ships in the river displayed their colours; houses at night were illuminated all over the city; and every decent and orderly method was observed to demonstrate the just sense they entertained of his Majesty's goodness, and the wisdom of Parliament, in conciliating the minds of the people on this critical occasion. . . .[12]

Indeed, the anniversary of the Stamp Act repeal continued to be the occasion of colorful displays, and of implicit political statements, for several years thereafter.

Nevertheless, the most usual groups to act in those years represented individual trades. Sometimes large ones. In a sequel to the petition we noticed earlier in *Gentleman's Magazine*, May 1765 brought repeated marches of the Spitalfields weavers. On the fourteenth, a "large body" assembled to a drumbeat and proceeded to St. James flying a black flag, only to discover that the king was away. On the sixteenth, some 8,000 marched from Morefields to St. James but were dispersed by the Guards. On the seventeenth, says the magazine,

> The Spittle Fields weavers assembled again, and appeared as a formidable body before the House of Peers, but committed no act of violence in that neighborhood. In their return home, the house of Mr. Carr and Cox, on Ludgate Hill, mercers, was beset, the windows broke, and other damage done, but whether by the weavers, or an indiscriminate mob, is not quite certain. However, on the approach of the civil and military power of the city, the rioters dispersed, and

---

[12] Ibid., 1766, p. 77. See also John Stevenson, "Food Riots in England, 1792–1818," in John Stevenson and Roland Quinault, eds., *Popular Protest and Public Order: Six Studies in British History, 1790–1920* (London: George Allen & Unwin, 1974); and Walter J. Shelton, *English Hunger and Industrial Disorders: A Study of Social Conflict during the First Decade of George III's Reign* (London: Macmillan, 1973). More general studies of eighteenth-century British crime and social turbulence include Douglas Hay *et al.*, *Albion's Fatal Tree: Crime and Society in Eighteenth-Century England* (New York: Pantheon, 1975); E. P. Thompson, *Whigs and Hunters: The Origin of the Black Act* (New York: Pantheon, 1975); and Leon Radzinowicz, *A History of English Criminal Law and Its Administration, vol. IV: Grappling for Control* (London: Stevens, 1968).

peace was restored. The pretence for this outrage was that the partners were encouragers of the importation of foreign silks. On the same day a great body of the people and others appeared before the Duke of Bedford's in Bloomsbury Square, where a party of horse and foot were sent to disperse them, on which occasion much mischief was done by the horse pressing among the mob, and trampling down all before them. By these proceedings, the whole city of London was in some measure alarmed, and the magistracy were vigilant to prevent bad consequences, orders were issued for the city militia to hold themselves in readiness at an hours warning; guards were placed at the most considerable avenues about town, and the justices published papers threatening rioters with the penalties of the law.[13]

The crowd had assembled at the Duke of Bedford's house because the Duke had "defeated a Bill designed to protect the London silk-weavers' livelihood by excluding French silks. . . ."[14] In response to the weavers' demands, the merchants associated to recall their foreign orders, and Parliament reimposed the tariff on foreign silks. This is still a defensive action, to some extent. But it is a defensive action on a scale and with a national political focus unmatched by any turnpike protest or food riot. Indeed, despite widespread poverty and frequent hunger, no food riots occurred in London during 1765 and 1766.

Other collective actions in London of those years were smaller and less manifestly political than the silkweaver's marches and the booksellers's pillory crowd. In 1765, for example, London's seamen and coalheavers struck and protested in response to a great conflict in the coalfields of the northeast. The silkweavers themselves often acted against particular masters to petition Parliament or attack the Duke of Bedford. On the average, nevertheless, the events of London stand out from those of the rest of England by their scale and their orientation to the national structure of power.

The contrast continued in 1774 and 1775, when English protest was at a lower level. In most of the country, the popular collective actions that attracted the attention of newspapers or

---

[13] *Gentleman's Magazine*, 1765, pp. 244–245. See also *Annual Register*, 1765, pp. 41–42.

[14] Rudé, *Hanoverian London*, p. 198.

magistrates were antienclosure movements, turnpike protests, and the like. In those years, the provinces were free of food riots but seem to have had more than the usual number of robberies by large bands of brigands. There were strikes, notably those of the shipwrights of Portsmouth (who were fighting the substitution of wage work for task work) and of the 800 or 900 weavers at Keighley, Yorkshire, where the workers went out for higher wages and destroyed the pieces of weavers who would not join the movement. Furthermore the cutting off of trade with the American colonies produced reactions in provincial England. One of the more surprising reactions occurred in the ports:

> The slave trade having been greatly affected by the late Order of Council for prohibiting the exportation of gunpowder, &c., the sailors of Liverpool, who are unemployed on that account, assembled in a body, and threatened destruction to the whole town. They had got several pieces of cannon, which they fired; but a party of light-horse being sent for from Manchester, they were soon dispersed, and about 40 of them lodged in gaol.[15]

A different reaction (but one that also stressed acute discontent with English conditions) appeared in the *Gentleman's Magazine* historical chronicle for September 23, 1775. "The ship Jupiter," the account read, "from Dunstaffnage Bay, with 200 emigrants on board, chiefly from Argyleshire, set sail for North Carolina. They declare the oppressions of their landlords are such that they can no longer submit to them." [16]

Although the provinces thus produced a number of indirect responses to the American crisis, only in London do we find a continuous, large-scale effort to influence royal policy concerning the colonies. Petitions, meetings, and debates about American policy filled the capital's public life in 1774 and 1775. It was the time of Burke's eloquent, ironic pleas for the American cause. (At one time he boasted that with respect to certain arguments in favor of retaining the tea tax he would "give such damning proof, that, however the contrary may be whispered in circles, or bawled in news papers, they never more will dare to raise their voices in

---

[15] *Gentleman's Magazine*, 1775, p. 450.
[16] Ibid., p. 496.

this House.") [17] In June 1774, the "Lord Mayor, Alderman and Commons of the City of London" petitioned the king against the Quebec Act; in June 1775 they went so far as to call for the people of London to march with them as they presented another petition against the repression of the American colonies.[18] In March 1775, when the "common hangman" burned copies of "The Crisis, NO. III" and a pamphlet "The Present Crisis with respect to America" at the Royal Exchange gate a "prodigious concourse of people" tried to keep the city marshal and the hangman from lighting the fire.[19] In June 1775 the Constitutional Society took up a subscription for "American widows and orphans" while in August a Committee of Correspondence formed to maintain contact with the Americans.[20]

In those years, London also witnessed the dénouement of the great Wilkite movement. The former prisoner, exile, and disqualified member of Parliament became Lord Mayor. Our two time periods miss the high points of Wilkism: John Wilkes' first imprisonment for criticism of royal policy occurred in 1763. His flight to France to avoid further prosecution followed soon after. In 1765, he was in exile, although such supporters as the pilloried bookseller we encountered earlier were keeping his name and program in view. The next great moments arrived in 1768 and 1769; mass marches first celebrated his election to Parliament, then protested his exclusion from Parliament. Wilkes became more identified with the American cause. When he and Serjeant Glynn stood for Parliament in the fall of 1774, the engagement they signed combined domestic and colonial concerns; they would strive, they said

[17] Ibid., 1774, p. 602.

[18] Public Record Office (London), State Papers of George III, 37/10–11 (hereinafter cited as P. R. O., S. P.).

[19] *Gentleman's Magazine*, 1775, p. 148.

[20] P. R. O., S. P., 37/11. General studies of eighteenth-century British reform efforts include John Cannon, *Parliamentary Reform, 1640–1832* (Cambridge: Cambridge University Press, 1973), and Caroline Robbins, *The Eighteenth-Century Commonwealthman* (Cambridge: Harvard University Press, 1959). A significant background study is C. B. Macpherson, *The Political Theory of Possessive Individualism: Hobbes to Locke* (Oxford: Clarendon Press, 1962).

to restore and defend the excellent form of government modelled and established at the Revolution, and to promote acts of the legislature for shortening the duration of parliaments, for excluding placemen and pensioners from the House of Commons; for a more fair and equal representation of the people; for vindication of the injured rights of the freeholders of this county, and the whole body of the electors of this united kingdom; and an act for the repeal of the four late acts respecting America; the Quebec act, establishing popery, and the system of French Canadian laws, in that extensive province; the Boston port-act, the act for altering the charter of the province of Massachusetts-Bay, and the act for the trial, in Europe, of persons accused of criminal offenses in America. . . .[21]

Launching an electoral campaign with a platform—especially this one—was an important innovation.

What is more, Wilkes' platform was popular. When after two setbacks Wilkes won the mayoralty of London in October 1774, *Gentleman's Magazine* reported:

On this occasion the joy of the populace was so great that they took the horses from the coach and, in the struggle for the honour of drawing it to the Mansion House, one man lost his life and another was much hurt.[22]

The eighth of October brought a curious sequel, curiously reported:

The Coroner's inquest sat on the body of the man who was trampled to death in attempting to assist in drawing the Lord Mayor's coach . . . and brought in their verdict Accidental Death. The law, nevertheless, exacts the forfeiture of the moving body towards the death of a subject; in consequence of which the jury adjudged the near fore-wheel of the Lord Mayor's coach the moving body, and valued the same at 40s.[23]

During the spring of 1775 the new mayor repeatedly petitioned Parliament and the king concerning national affairs. In June,

21 *Gentleman's Magazine*, 1774, p. 444.
22 Ibid., p. 491.
23 Ibid.

59

Wilkes figured in the presentation to the king of a petition which the solicitor general considered to be seditious libel. It began

> Resolved, that whoever advised his Majesty to declare that we would not in future receive on the throne any address, remonstrance, and petition from the Lord Mayor, Alderman, and Livery of London are enemies of the right of the subject to petition the throne; because such advice is calculated to intercept the complaints of the people to their Sovereign, to prevent a redress of grievances, and alienate the minds of Englishmen from the Hanoverian succession.[24]

As it happens, the unacceptable petitions protested British policy in America.

In this period, no great change in the overall patterns of popular collective action appeared outside of London. In the metropolis itself, however, three significant alterations were in progress. A well-defined Radical movement, largely middle class but allied with leaders of the city's skilled crafts, was gaining strength and pressing for political reform. The Spitalfields silkweavers and other crafts were moving toward large-scale labor organization and simultaneous pressure on the masters and the government. The movements were refashioning the available repertoires of collective action. Around the old right of petitioning Parliament and the king, for example, the supporters of Wilkes began organizing something like the modern demonstration, with its massing in the name of some particular interest, its deliberate display of symbols, slogans, and demands, and its intentional deployment of a crowd near the premises of the people its leaders wished to criticize or influence. In the London crowd of the later eighteenth century, we begin to see the forms of popular collective action that would prevail in the nineteenth and twentieth centuries. In their eighteenth-century setting, they were striking innovations.

III. Actions in Massachusetts

Innovations were appearing in the American colonies as well. The general flow of events in Massachusetts is well known, since

[24] P. R. O., S. P., 37/11.

they play such an important part in the general history of the revolution.[25] Our periods take us from the Stamp Act resistance of 1765 to the armed conflicts of 1775. Work by historians on urban colonial crowds has given us a better grasp of the social context of famous events and of the relation of Massachusetts' ordinary people to them.[26] Well before 1765, it turns out, they were resisting the pressures of the market and the state in much the manner of their English contemporaries. If the reports in such publications as the *Boston Gazette* are any sign, they maintained a lively interest in the mother country's own conflicts—food riots, the marches of the Spitalfields weavers, the campaigns of John Wilkes all pass in review.

The mixture of issues in America, however, was different. Although Massachusetts produced some food riots resembling those of provincial England, in that maritime province the most

[25] See, especially, Bernard Bailyn, *The Ordeal of Thomas Hutchinson* (Cambridge: Harvard University Press, 1974); Bernard Knollenberg, *Origins of the American Revolution: 1759–1766*, revised edition, (New York: Free Press, 1965); Alan Rogers, *Empire and Liberty: American Resistance to British Authority, 1755–1763* (Berkeley: University of California Press, 1974), Chapters. 4–7, *passim*; Pauline R. Maier, *From Resistance to Revolution: Colonial Radicals and the Development of American Opposition to Britain, 1765–1776* (New York: Alfred A. Knopf, 1972); Gary B. Nash, "Social Change and the Growth of Prerevolutionary Urban Radicalism," pp. 3–36, in Young, *American Revolution*; and Alfred F. Young, "Pope's Day, Tar and Feathers, and 'Cornet Joyce, Jun.': From Ritual to Rebellion in Boston, 1745–1775" (unpublished paper, Anglo-American Labor Historians' Conference, Rutgers University, 1973).

[26] For example, Jesse Lemisch, "The American Revolution Seen from the Bottom Up," pp. 3–45, in Barton J. Bernstein, ed., *Towards a New Past: Dissenting Essays in American History* (New York: Pantheon, 1968); and Jesse Lemisch and John K. Alexander, "The White Oaks, Jack Tar, and the Concept of the 'Inarticulate'," *William and Mary Quarterly*, 3rd ser., 29 (1972): 109–142. On revolutionary era turbulence, in general, see Carl Bridenbaugh, *Cities in Revolt: Urban Life in America, 1743–1776* (New York: Capricorn Books, 1965); Richard Maxwell Brown, *Strain of Violence: Historical Studies of American Violence and Vigilantism* (New York: Oxford University Press, 1975), Chapter 2; Robert Cecil, "Oligarchy and Mob-Rule in the American Revolution," *History Today*, 13 (1963): 197–204; Richard B. Morris, "Class Struggle and the American Revolution," *William and Mary Quarterly*, 3rd ser., 19 (1962): 3–29; Richard A. Ryerson, "Political Mobilization and the American Revolution: The Resistance Movement in Philadelphia, 1765 to 1776," *William and Mary Quarterly*, 3rd ser., 23 (1966): 635–642. A broader treatment is Kenneth A. Lockridge, "Social Change and the Meaning of the American Revolution," *Journal of Social History*, 6 (1973): 403–439.

significant causes of aggressive crowd action were the rivalries of adjacent settlements, impressment for naval service, the crown's commandeering of pine trees for masts, and the enforcement of customs regulations.

The clashes over customs accelerated after the peace of 1763, when the British tightened their surveillance as part of the general effort to increase the revenue from the colonies. The high cost of the war and the expense of maintaining troops in and around Britain's greatly enlarged colonial domain motivated the search for new revenue. The Stamp Act belonged to the same effort. Its chief opponents in Massachusetts, however, were not the smugglers and small coastal traders who had spearheaded the earlier resistance to customs regulations, but a coalition of merchants and artisans concentrated in Boston.

In general, the great merchants favored moderate legal action, while the artisans were readier to take to the streets against the stamp distributors. The link between the two was the group of patriots around Samuel Adams. They were then called the Loyal Nine, later they provided the nucleus of the Sons of Liberty. The Loyal Nine helped arrange an alliance between the usually hostile factions of craftsmen from the North End and the South End, uniting them in an attack on the "placemen" who were to benefit from the administration of the Stamp Act.

Threats and resistance began weeks before the famous actions of August twenty-sixth. Much of the popular collective action used the same sort of street theater we have seen in English actions of the time. For example, on the fourteenth of August, says the *Boston Gazette and Country Journal,*

> the Effigy of a Gentleman sustaining a very unpopular Office, that of St__p Master, was found hanging on a Tree in the most public Part of the Town, together with a Boot, wherein was concealed a young Imp of the D__l represented as peeping out of the Top—On the Breast of the Effigy was a Label in Praise of Liberty, and denouncing Vengeance on the Subverters of it. . . .[27]

The crowd stopped the tree's owner from taking down the effigy

[27] *Boston Gazette,* August 19, 1765. In the revolutionary period the title of the *Boston Gazette* varies slightly.

by threatening damage to his house. All day the demonstrators required everyone carrying goods to market to have them stamped by the effigy. They prevented the sheriff's effort to remove the dummies. The enthusiastic crowd numbered in the thousands. At dusk, a large procession, included a phalanx of master craftsmen, drew the dummy of Lord Bute around Boston on a bier, demolished a new building said to be meant for a stamp office, broke a few windows at the designated stamp collector's house, beheaded and burned the dummy, again attacked Andrew Oliver's house, returned to the bonfire and ended the day by stoning Lieutenant Governor Hutchinson and Sheriff Greenleaf, who came to disperse them.[28] The fateful tree which bore Lord Bute came to be known as Liberty Tree. It became the model for the liberty trees all over America, and eventually, for one of the standard revolutionary symbols in France during its own revolution 25 years later. This action against Andrew Oliver was the first visible work of the crucial alliance between the mechanics of the North End and the South End, fostered by the efforts of the Loyal Nine.[29]

Popular attacks on the Stamp Act and its reputed defenders continued until repeal the following spring. *Gentleman's Magazine* has already told us about the sacking of Hutchinson's mansion, 12 days after the raid on Andrew Oliver's. There were more, although none of them reached so high and so far. As the Stamp Act took effect on November 1, according to the *Boston Gazette*, bells tolled, ships' flags flew at half mast, and Liberty Tree bore effigies of George Grenville and John Huske, the British Minister and the American-born Member of Parliament. After parading the effigies around town in a cart and stringing them up for a while on the gallows,

> the Populace, in token of their utter Detestation of the Men they were designed to represent, tore them in pieces and flung their Limbs with Indignation into the Air. This being done, three Cheers were given, and every Man was desired to repair to his Home. . . .[30]

Similar actions, on a smaller scale, terrorized the potential stamp

[28] Hoerder, *Crowd Action*, pp. 97–101.
[29] Ibid., pp. 93–96.
[30] *Boston Gazette*, November 4, 1765.

distributors throughout Massachusetts. Many resigned publicly before large crowds. There was much posting of threatening notices and burning of effigies.

At the time of a call for public bonfires of stamps in February 1766, a stage and gallows appeared under Liberty Tree. This time the impresarios hung up effigies of Bute, Grenville, and the Devil, placed a chained image of a stamp in the dock, and carried out a mock trial before a crowd of 2000 or 3000. Gallows humor, literally. "After many learned debates," reports the *Boston Gazette*, "the Evidence was so clear, that the Jury without going out of Court found the said Prisoner guilty of a Breach of Magna Charta, and a Design to subvert the British Constitution, and alienate the affections of His Majesty's most loyal and dutiful Subjects in America from his Person and Government." [31] The people's court sentenced the effigies to be paraded through the streets and burned beneath the gallows. In Salem, Marblehead, Falmouth, Casco Bay, and Plymouth, similar scenarios were acted out.

In this case and many others, Boston led, but the rest of Massachusetts was close behind. Outside of Boston, the crowds often attacked class enemies—creditors and exploiters. With such a degree of political sensitivity and coordination, one might say that the Revolution began in 1765. Whether that is right or not depends on what is meant by "revolution." But a leap to 1774 shows that Massachusetts had further steps to take on the road to open rebellion.

In 1774, following the Boston Tea Party, public burning or dunking of British tea became a regular happening in the colony. Tarring and feathering of Tories and royal officials likewise became common. The greatest alteration, however, came with the impact of the Intolerable Acts—the occupation and closing of the port of Boston in order to force the city back into compliance with Britain. With the arrival of occupying troops in the summer of 1774 began a campaign of passive, then active, resistance that led step by step to armed struggle the following year. A general reaction against the troops and finally against almost all royal institutions did a major part of the revolutionary work. Bostonians

[31] Ibid., February 24, 1766.

organized a campaign to encourage the desertion of British troops.[32] The courts closed. People's courts took their place. In Springfield, at the scheduled opening of the royal court in August 1774, large bodies of men marched into town from the surrounding region, occupied the court, and began their own trials of accused Tories. As an eyewitness reported,

> No man received the least injury, but the strictest order of justice were observed. The people to their honor behaved with the greatest order and regularity, a few individuals excepted, and avoided, as much as possible, confusion. The people of each town being drawn into separate companies marched with staves and musick. The trumpets sounding, drums beating, fifes playing and Colours flying, struck the passions of the soul into a proper tone, and inspired martial courage into each.[33]

Massachusetts' middle-class leaders resisted and feared such movements when the movements lacked the proper middle-class leadership. But the net effects of boycott, coordination, and crowd pressure were to isolate the British troops and the Tories from any local support and to build a set of parallel institutions of government through town meetings, committees of correspondence, and vigilante groups. The most dramatic encounters were yet to come —at Lexington, Concord, and elsewhere. Yet with that parallel government, a truly revolutionary situation had developed.

IV. Actions in South Carolina

Collective action in South Carolina is not so well documented for this period. The affairs of the 1750s and 1760s in the colony nevertheless make it clear that South Carolina was quite a different place from Massachusetts. South Carolina was a much newer colony than Massachusetts, essentially an eighteenth-century cre-

---

[32] Public Record Office (London), Colonial Office Papers, 5/120 (hereafter cited as P. R. O., C. O.).

[33] Hoerder, *Crowd Action*, p. 283-4. On Boston, see also Michael S. Hindus, "A City of Mobocrats and Tyrants: Mob Violence in Boston, 1741–1863, *Issues in Criminology*, 6 (1971) : 55-83.

ation. South Carolina divided into a few commercialized ports, notably the metropolis of Charleston; a nearby area of plantations worked with slave labor; a large frontier region combining clusters of small farmers with Indian enclaves; and a major zone still dominated by Indian hunters and gatherers, penetrated only by scattered military outposts and a few French and English traders, trappers, and farmers. Much of the governmental business consisted of creating or maintaining alliances with the Choctaws, Chickasaws, Cherokees, and Creeks while trying to make sure that the French did not do the same.

The governors of South Carolina also found themselves trying to keep the frontier from moving west faster than their means of administration, communication, and military intervention could expand. Among the British settlers, one of the most acute political divisions resulted from the demands of the people in distant frontier settlements. They insisted that the authorities in Charleston either provide courts and other governmental institutions at the frontier or allow the frontiersmen to create their own. That conflict swelled in the 1760s to a series of small rebellions and the vigilante activities of the South Carolina Regulators.[34]

South Carolina's large black slave population produced numerous runaways, and an occasional threat of rebellion, as at the time of 1765's Christmas festivities. Later on, Lieutenant Governor William Bull reported:

> As I had received accounts that 107 Negroes had left their Plantations soon after the intended Insurrection had been discovered, and joined a large number of Runaways in Colleton County which might increase to a formidable Body, I thought it very advisable to call down some of the Catawbas as Indians strike Terrour into the Negroes, and the

---

[34] Richard Maxwell Brown, *The South Carolina Regulators* (Cambridge: Harvard University Press, 1963). Additional works on South Carolina turbulence in the Revolutionary period include Pauline R. Maier, "The Charleston Mob and the Evolution of Popular Politics in Revolutionary South Carolina, 1765-1784," *Perspectives in American History*, 4 (1970): 173-196; Jerome Nadelhaft, "The Revolutionary Era in South Carolina, 1775-1788" (Ph.D. dissertation, University of Wisconsin, Madison, 1965); George C. Rogers, Jr., "The Charleston Tea Party: The Significance of December 3, 1773," *South Carolina Historical Magazine*, 75 (1974): 153-168; and Richard Walsh, *Charleston's Sons of Liberty* (Columbia: University of South Carolina Press, 1959).

Indians manner of hunting render them more sagacious in tracking and expert in finding out the hidden recesses, where the Runaways conceal themselves from the Usual searches of the English and also that the Negroes may see that the Indians are easily to be brought down upon them. . . .[35]

As compared with Massachusetts, then, much more of South Carolina's governmental energy normally went into controlling, dividing, and conquering hostile populations.

In 1765 and 1766, however, the Stamp Act dominated South Carolina's politics as it did the politics of Massachusetts. The *South Carolina Gazette* packed its pages with news of Stamp Act resistance elsewhere in the colonies. In general, South Carolina's own response was the response of Charleston's merchants and artisans; it was a relatively cautious response, but it hardened into resistance there as elsewhere. On the eighteenth of October 1765, the ship *Planter's Adventure* sailed into Charleston Harbor with the official stamped paper on board. "Early on Saturday morning," reports the *Gazette,*

in the middle of Broad Street and Church Street, near Mr. Dillon's . . . appeared suspended on a gallows twenty feet high, an effigy, with a figure of the devil on its right hand, and on its left a boot, with a head stuck upon it distinguished by a blue bonnet, to each of which were affixed labels expressive of the sense of the people in their loyalty but tenacious of just liberty. They declared that all internal duties imposed upon them without the consent of their immediate or even virtual representation was grievous, oppressive, and unconstitutional, and that an extension of the powers and jurisdiction of admiralty courts in America tended to subvert one of their most darling legal rights, that of trial by juries.[36]

If we had not already been to Massachusetts, we might be surprised to find such elaborate constitutional arguments tacked to a gallows. Yet the whole proceeding expressed a clear, precise, even legalistic sense of grievance. Another sign attached to the

---

[35] South Carolina Archives Department (Columbia), Commons House of Assembly Journal, January 14, 1766.
[36] *South Carolina Gazette* (Charleston), October 31, 1765.

gallows read "LIBERTY AND NO STAMP ACT," and threatened anyone who tore down the grim structure.

Saturday evening a crowd came with a procession of wagons displaying gallows, signs, and effigies. They paraded to the house of George Saxby, the designated stamp distributor, which was currently occupied by a Captain Coats. There the crowd broke a few windows and opened the house to ask for stamped papers. None were in the house. The paraders moved to the town green, then to the barracks, where they burned the effigies. Someone rang the bells of Saint Michael's Church. Later on, Saxby declared that he was not going to distribute the stamps. He even claimed that he had never really been appointed.

South Carolina continued more cautiously than Massachusetts, but South Carolina continued. As in Massachusetts, the Stamp Act repeal and its anniversaries were occasions for major public celebrations; by 1774, significantly, the chief pageant was a display of the might and discipline of the new companies of provincial militia. In the later 1760s, Charleston adopted many of the standard forms of American patriotism: organization of a John Wilkes club, meetings and ceremonies at the city's own Liberty Tree, and so on. Charleston's artisans and a few allies among the merchants became the activists of the local Sons of Liberty. The assembly moved into a bitter struggle with the governor over the rights to tax, appoint, and issue money in the colony. With some reluctance, Charleston's merchants adopted and enforced nonimportation agreements; according to Lieutenant Governor Bull's reports, they were largely effective by 1769.[37]

Nonetheless, 1774 brought a great increase in the tempo and range of South Carolina's mobilization against the British. On July sixth, for example, gathered what the *Gazette* called "the LARGEST BODY of the *most respectable Inhabitants* that had ever been seen together on any public Occasion *here,* or perhaps anywhere in America" to adopt resolutions condemning the tea tax, the Intolerable Acts, the trial of Americans in England—essentially the same *syllabus errorum* that meetings of Bostonians and Londoners were preparing at the same time. By November, Charlestonians were dumping and burning tea like their northern brethern. On Pope's Day, the effigies on display included not only the Devil and the Pope, but also Lord North and Thomas Hutchinson. The sign over their heads read "ROBBERS ARE WHITE-ROB'D SAINTS, COMPAR'D TO TYRANTS. MAGNA CHARTA, AND THE OATHS OF KINGS, ARE COBWEBS NOW; WITNESS, THE VIOLATION OF THE BOSTON CHARTER." [38]

The boycott and individual pressure against South Carolina's Tories and royal officials intensified in 1774 to the point of producing nearly separate societies and parallel governments. On August 14, 1775, the General Committee issued a solemn prohibition of "Correspondence, Intercourse or Dealing" between signers and nonsigners of the act of association against Great Britain.[39] Just after, Charleston's postmaster wrote that

> Persecution continues to go on against the Friends and Officers of Government without intermission, or the most distant prospect of relief from any quarter. . . . All officers and others who had refused to sign the Association were again called upon the 15th instant before the Committees, when they were called in one by one and ask'd if they would take the following oath: "I, AB, Do solemnly swear upon the Holy Evangelist of Almighty God, that during the present disputes between Great Britain and America, I will not directly, by Deed, word or writing, attempt to counteract or oppose the proceedings of the People in North America. . . ." [40]

To be sure, we can put South Carolina in perspective by recalling that by then the people of Massachusetts were not simply operating parallel governments but engaging in open warfare against British troops. South Carolina lagged behind Massachusetts.

Indeed, the later history of the Revolution revealed important differences between South Carolina and Massachusetts. Most important, in South Carolina the Tories remained fairly strong outside of Charleston itself. Four years after the Declaration of Independence, the correspondence of royal Lieutenant Governor Bull shows him to be mildly hopeful, despite the terrible struggles of previous years, about regaining his lost property and position

[38] *South Carolina Gazette*, July 11, November 21, 1774.
[39] Ibid., September 7, 1775.
[40] P. R. O., C. O., 5/386.

in the colony. In 1780 and 1781, a bloody war between loyalists and patriots tore up the South Carolina back country. Nevertheless, the most remarkable feature of South Carolina's collective action from 1765 to 1775 is its convergence with the forms and objectives of action elsewhere in the American colonies. That convergence, we have seen, extended to the use of the same symbols and rituals to dramatize the political choices being made.

V. Conclusions

If we return to our earlier concept, thinking of Massachusetts and South Carolina as remote English counties, and compare them with real English counties during the same decade, what do we find? First, some intriguing similarities: the general use of ritual, symbols, and drama in crowd action; the regularity with which popular collective action consisted of ordinary people's taking over the roles and procedures of the constituted authorities; the salience of well-defined questions of rights; the generally reactive character of the claims being made. All these are standard features of eighteenth-century popular collective action. They appear not only in England and its American colonies but in the European world as a whole.

Further similarities between England and America resulted from mutual communication within a common political tradition. We have seen Americans paying attention to John Wilkes, Englishmen protesting about the Intolerable Acts. The indirect alliance between London radicals and American patriots expressed a common bourgeois interest in parliamentary representation and power. As E. P. Thompson has long since insisted for eighteenth-century England, ordinary people on both sides of the Atlantic seem to have taken the right of freeborn Englishmen to be genuine, inalienable, and rooted in a constitution.[41]

Yet, there are also important differences. First, it appears that

[41] E. P. Thompson, "The Moral Economy of the English Crowd in the Eighteenth Century," *Past and Present*, 50 (February, 1971): 76–136, and *The Making of the English Working Class* (London: John Gollancz, 1963).

in America from 1765 to 1775 the entire range of collective action became tied directly to the division between loyalists and patriots. The political polarization realigned lesser political conflicts. If we may reason by analogy with French, Russian, and Chinese experiences, this absorption of all conflicts into a single conflict is a crucial marker of a deeply revolutionary situation. In America we see that revolutionary process absorbing all other political processes. In England, especially outside of London, we have, by contrast, seen the standard food riots, turnpike conflicts, and struggles over enclosures proceeding more or less independently of the radical movement in London.

Second, in America we find deliberately formed associations such as the Sons of Liberty linking, and sometimes even organizing, a wide range of popular and elite collective actions. In that regard, the colonists again resembled the London radicals more than they did provincial Englishmen.

Third, from 1765 to 1775 we discover among the Americans a continuously high level of mobilization, of sensitivity, of readiness for action. Again, London radicalism bears some resemblance to the American situation, but the comparison sets off America quite sharply from England as a whole.

Finally, in America we witness the elaboration of a parallel set of institutions—committees of correspondence, people's courts, and others—which have no equivalent in that England where crowds and elites kept trying to influence king, Parliament, and local gentry but not to do without them. In that construction of a potential government outside the British colonial government lay the preparation of a genuine revolution.

The American Revolution, as Robert R. Palmer has reminded us, stood for several decades as the chief exemplar, the favorite European symbol, of the possibility of liberation from oppressive, arbitrary governments.[42] The multiplicity of the revolutionary institutions and their orientation to the protection of local rights apparently reinforced the decentralization of Ameri-

[42] Robert R. Palmer, "The Fading Dream: How European Revolutionaries Have Seen the American Revolution," in Bede Lackner and Kenneth R. Philip, eds., *Essays on Modern European Revolutionary History* ("The Walter Prescott Webb Memorial Lectures") (Austin: University of Texas Press, forthcoming).

can government and blocked that rush of power toward the new state which is common in thoroughgoing revolutions. Despite important class division with respect to interests and collective action, the American Revolution appears to have transferred power within the bourgeoisie rather than bringing about the realignment of classes we can reasonably attribute to the French, Russian, and Chinese revolutions. The analogy of the American experience to England's seventeenth-century revolutions is as good as its analogy to the European revolutions of 1789, 1848, or 1917. But if America's eighteenth-century revolution did seventeenth-century work in struggling against the demands of a centralizing, war-making state, it did so by means of collective action that was fully of its own century and pointed toward the expanded scale of mobilization and action which would be characteristic of the following century. At least that is how the American experience looks from the vantage point of Europe in the seventeenth, eighteenth, and nineteenth centuries. In its purposes and consequences, the American Revolution primarily clung to the past. In the means employed, it stood at the leading edge of social change.

ACKNOWLEDGMENTS

In preparing this essay I wish to acknowledge the valuable advice of John Dann, Charles Lee, and Charles Lesser; the enthusiastic and intelligent aid of Martha Guest, R. A. Schweitzer, and David Weir, and the editorial suggestions of Louise Tilly. The financial support of the National Science Foundation is also gratefully acknowledged as are comments by audiences at Hollins College and Indiana University who heard earlier versions of this essay.

4

Back Country Rebellions and the Homestead Ethic in America, 1740-1799

Richard Maxwell Brown

In the broad sweep of the period of the American Revolution there were not just one but two pathways of rebellion. One was the movement against Britain that led to the American Revolution. The other was a pathway of disparate, localized popular rebellions occurring in the rural back country of America. There were nine such violent rebellions from 1740 to 1799, enlisting, in sum, at least 21,000 participants with perhaps another 25,000 nonparticipating sympathizers. The focus on the American Revolution has diverted attention from the back country popular rebellions. Although the nine rebellions have been treated individually, there has been no attempt to consider all of them together—to determine whether, despite diversity, they exhibit a transcendent unity of causation, action, and result. In addition, there is an important problem common to the task of interpreting the American Revolution and the challenge of understanding the nine back country rebellions—the problem of social conflict. Did the back country rebellions constitute, overall, a social revolution?

I. The Land–Population–Wealth Crisis

Before addressing, briefly, the problem of social conflict, it is well to note the one thing that seems more than any other to have structured social reality for Americans, both urban and rural, in the middle and late eighteenth century—the land–population–wealth crisis.[1] The crisis resulted primarily from the combination of the fastest growing population in the Western world with a limited, nonexpanding land base restricted to the relatively narrow belt of the 13 colonies along the Atlantic coast. The result of the combination of a stationary land base with a populace that doubled every generation was extreme population pressure on the land. The outcome—as depicted in the work of Lockridge, Henretta, Kulikoff, Nash, and others—was a strong tendency for both the urban and rural lower and middle classes to suffer a notable decline, absolute or relative, in wealth and property. Conversely, there was a pronounced trend of increasing affluence for the upper class—the most prosperous 30% of the population.[2] Hence, the paradoxical result of booming eighteenth-century American economic growth was a mixture of gainers and losers among a people characterized on the whole by declining per capita wealth. To put it baldly, the poor got poorer, the rich got richer, and those in between declined in relative wealth or, at best, only held their own. Headed by Gary B. Nash, some historians have recently argued incisively that it was the absolute or relative decline of the

[1] The land–population–wealth crisis has best been explored by Kenneth A. Lockridge in two classic articles: "Land, Population, and the Evolution of New England Society, 1630–1790," *Past and Present*, April 1968, and "Social Change and the Meaning of the American Revolution," *Journal of Social History*, 6 (1972–73): 403–439.

[2] Lockridge, "Social Change," pp. 407–408; James Henretta, "Economic Development and Social Structure in Colonial Boston," *William and Mary Quarterly*, 3rd ser., 22 (1965): 75–92; Allan Kulikoff, "The Progress of Inequality in Revolutionary Boston," *William and Mary Quarterly*, 3rd ser., 28 (1971): 375–412; Gary B. Nash, "Social Change and the Growth of Revolutionary Urban Radicalism," pp. 3–36, in Alfred F. Young, ed., *The American Revolution* (DeKalb: Northern Illinois University Press, 1976) and "Urban Wealth and Poverty in Pre-Revolutionary America," *Journal of Interdisciplinary History*, 6 (1975–76): 545–584.

urban lower and middle classes that energized the American revolutionary movement.[3]

If, then, the situation in the late colonial cities exemplified a narrow elite, top-heavy with riches, then why did not a social revolution occur in conjunction with the American Revolution? Why did not the depressed, lower and middle classes, in relative decline, turn against the ultra-affluent upper-class merchants and professionals who thrived so strikingly on the trend toward more narrowly held wealth? Why was the mob violence of Boston and other cities directed not against the indigenous urban aristocracy but at British officials, military personnel, and their supporters? One answer is that, although the lower-class urban rioters of the revolutionary period had pressing reasons to revolt, they simply lacked the ideology to do so. The urban crowds possessed no doctrine of lower-class rebellion in their preindustrial age. Instead the revolutionary ideology—as delineated by Bernard Bailyn and others—was such as to cause the hard-pressed urbanites to perceive and resent an external enemy, the British, rather than an internal enemy composed of more economically fortunate Americans. Thus, American city dwellers rioted against British policy and its supporters.

Extreme social conflict in revolutionary America occurred in the rural back country areas of the countryside rather than in the cities. In the back country, discontent was comparable to that occurring in the cities. Although the growing gap between the rich and the poor was not as great in rural America, it was nevertheless significant. Increasing population pressure on the land meant that more and more rural Americans could not hope to own farms. As population pressure in the old, settled farming areas closest to the coast increased, there was a natural tendency for land hungry ruralites to move toward the frontier. But not all went well in the back country, for the factor of eighteenth-century population pressure—especially after 1730—meant that more and more Americans competed for land in the back country as well as

[3] Nash, "Social Change" and "Urban Wealth and Poverty."

elsewhere.[4] As time passed, rising tax burdens and more onerous debt structures made life in the back country difficult for the small- and medium-scale farmers who made up the bulk of the population and would be the main participants in the back country rebellions.

II. The Homestead Ethic in the Back Country

Yet, unlike their lower- and middle-class counterparts in the cities, the depressed inhabitants of the back country responded with outright rebellion against their oppressors. Rebellions occurred in the back country, because the *homestead ethic* provided a basis for rebellion. The word *homestead,* although associated primarily with the rise of the free-land movement in the middle nineteenth century, was actually in use among colonial Americans as far back as 1638 to refer to the dwelling of a rural family with its associated land plot and outbuildings.[5] By the middle of the eighteenth century, the homestead ethic had matured as a cluster of values that characterized rural life. It included three key beliefs: in the right to have and hold, incontestably, a family-size farm; in the right to enjoy a homestead unencumbered by a ruinous economic burden; and in the right peacefully to occupy the homestead without fear of violence to person and property.

Crèvecoeur reflected the emotional attachment of rural Amer-

---

[4] James T. Lemon and Gary B. Nash, "The Distribution of Wealth in Eighteenth-Century America: A Century of Change in Chester County, Pennsylvania, 1693–1802," *Journal of Social History,* 1 (1967–1968) : 1–24; Robert A. Gross, *The Minutemen and Their World* (New York: Hill and Wang, 1976) ; Duane E. Ball, "Dynamics of Population and Wealth in Eighteenth-Century Chester County, Pennsylvania," *Journal of Interdisciplinary History,* 6 (1975–76) : 621–644; Lockridge, "Social Change," p. 414. One of the first of recent scholars to call attention to population density as a structuring factor for back country discontent was Charles S. Grant, *Democracy in the Connecticut Frontier Town of Kent* (New York: Columbia University Press, 1961) , p. 170.

[5] *Dictionary of Americanisms on Historical Principles, s. v.,* also citing examples of the use of the word in 1704, 1715, and 1749. J. Hector St. John de Crèvecoeur used the word in *Letters from an American Farmer,* 1782, (London: J. M. Dent, 1912) , p. 71.

icans to the homestead. "The instant I enter on my own land," he wrote, "the bright idea of property, of exclusive right, of independence exalts my mind." Declaring that all his "principal pleasures" were "centered within" the "scanty limits" of his homestead, Crevècoeur asked, "what should we American farmers be without the distinct possession of [the] soil?" His answer was direct and strong: "It feeds, it clothes us, from it we draw even a great exuberancy, our best meat, our richest drink," and—carried away with passion—"the very honey of our bees comes from this privileged spot" of earth.[6] With a background in the imported English yeoman tradition,[7] the homestead ethic yet grew more significantly out of the intrinsic American colonial custom of widespread landholding. From the very first generation of settlement in New England, "free public land grants" by the towns assured nearly all males of easy access to the land.[8] As Sumner Chilton Powell observed of the earliest seventeenth-century settlers of Sudbury, Massachusetts, "for the first time in their lives, the inhabitants of an English town were assuming that each adult male would be granted some land free and clear"—"a virtual social revolution"

[6] Crèvecoeur, *Letters*, pp. 23–24. In the *Letters* and in *Sketches of Eighteenth Century America*, ed. Henri L. Bourdin, Ralph H. Gabriel, and Stanley T. Williams (New Haven: Yale University Press, 1925), Crèvecoeur presents beneath the romantic flights of his prose able positivistic sketches of the processes of back country settlement, land gaining, and cultivation. Both works are suffused with the homestead ethic and its jeopardy in the late eighteenth century. See *Letters*, the first three letters and pp. 200–201, 230–231, and *Sketches*, pp. 62–151, 192–249. Pp. 26–70 and 89–92 of the *Sketches* reflect, implicitly, the land–population–wealth crisis. A provocative study dealing with the issue of land in late colonial America (but one that does not emphasize the range of back country rebellions explored here) is Rowland Berthoff and John M. Murrin, "Feudalism, Communalism, and the Yeoman Freeholder . . .," pp. 256–288, in Stephen G. Kurtz and James H. Hutson, eds., *Essays on the American Revolution* (Chapel Hill: University of North Carolina Press, 1973).

[7] Mildred L. Campbell, *The English Yeoman under Elizabeth and the Early Stuarts* (New Haven: Yale University Press, 1942).

[8] Kenneth A. Lockridge, *A New England Town: the First Hundred Years: Dedham, Massachusetts, 1636–1736* (New York: W. W. Norton, 1970), pp. 70–71. Richard L. Bushman, *From Puritan to Yankee: Character and the Social Order in Connecticut, 1690–1765* (Cambridge: Harvard University Press, 1967), pp. 34–35, 41–42, 49. Philip J. Greven, Jr., *Four Generations: Population, Land, and Family in Colonial Andover, Massachusetts* (Ithaca: Cornell University Press, 1970), Chapter 3.

compared to the old-country practice.[9] Extensive holding of land also prevailed in the middle and southern colonies where, under the headright system, free grants of 50 or more acres amounted to a de facto homestead system for farming families.[10] Thus, Richard P. McCormick's conclusion that in colonial New Jersey "it was not difficult for any man to acquire a homestead of his own" applies generally to the British provinces in America.[11]

Embedded in the exceptionally permissive custom of colonial landholding, therefore, was the belief—widespread in the revolutionary era and earlier—that "peaceable Possession, especially of back waste vacant Lands, is a Kind of Right"—a right entwined with "the common Method" of settling the land "time out of Mind" from "New-England to Georgia": the practice of "the Poor . . . always countenanced and approved of . . . to move out, from the interior Parts to the back Lands, with their Families and [to] find a Spot, whereon they might build "a Hut" and make "some Improvements." [12] Thus established on the land, the homesteader, by bestowing "his Labour on it," had gained the right to hold it without legal challenge, for from him, the land—so New Jerseymen asserted in 1746—"cannot be taken, without breaking thro' the Rule of Natural Justice; for thereby he would be actually deprived of the Fruits of his Industry." [13] Less direct than a legal threat to the status of the landholder but just as damaging in ultimate result were the dangers posed, on the one hand, by a crushing economic weight whether public or private, or, on the other, by the danger of violence. In regard to the latter threat—violence— the colonial homesteaders compared their right of peaceable

[9] Sumner Chilton Powell, *Puritan Village* (Middletown, Conn.: Wesleyan University Press, 1966) , pp. 83–88.

[10] David F. Hawke, *The Colonial Experience* (Indianapolis: Bobbs-Merrill, 1966) , pp. 100, 214, 234, 244, 375, 499.

[11] Richard P. McCormick, *New Jersey from Colony to State, 1609–1789* (Princeton: Van Nostrand, 1964) , pp. 25, 45, 55.

[12] Hermon Husband, *An Impartial Relation of the First Rise and Cause of the Recent Differences in Publick Affairs, in the Province of North Carolina . . .* (1770) , reprinted in William S. Powell, James K. Huhta, and Thomas J. Farnham, eds., *The Regulators in North Carolina: A Documentary History: 1759–1776* (Raleigh: North Carolina State Department of Archives and History, 1971) , p. 223.

[13] *New York Weekly Post-Boy*, June 9, 1746, quoted in Irving Mark, *Agrarian Conflicts in Colonial New York* (New York: Columbia University Press, 1940) , p. 140.

possession in America to the image of the languishing, endangered peasants of continental Europe: in contrast to the hapless husbandmen of *"Hungary* or *Germany"* who were condemned to live "in a State of War—continually exposed to the Incursions of *Hussars* and *Pandours,"* every American settler was entitled to sit "in Peace and Security under his own Vine, and his own Fig Tree." [14] But violent men were not the only danger to the secure occupancy of the farm, for "extortionate" public officials and privaté persons had the evil capacity to make the "whole properties" of "Our selves" and our "Innocent helpless Neighbours" a hostage to "utter Ruin" with the social consequences likely to be "wooden Shoes and uncombed Hair" in the supposed manner of the oppressed French peasantry.[15]

III.   The Goals of the Rebels

In chronological order the nine back country rebel movements were

1.   The New Jersey antiproprietary land rioters of the 1740s and 1750s [16]
2.   The New York antirent rioters of 1753–1766 [17]

[14] Richard J. Hooker, ed., *The Carolina Backcountry on the Eve of the Revolution: The Journal and other Writings of Charles Woodmason, Anglican Itinerant* (Chapel Hill: University of North Carolina Press, 1953), p. 214.

[15] Protest of Orange County, North Carolina, petitioners, October 19, 1770, in Powell, Huhta, and Farnham, *Regulators in North Carolina*, pp. 268–272.

[16] Gary S. Horowitz, "New Jersey Land Riots, 1745–1755" (Ph.D. dissertation, Ohio State University, 1966); Edward Countryman, "'Out of the Bounds of the Law': Northern Land Rioters in the Eighteenth Century," pp. 37–69, in Young, *American Revolution*; Donald L. Kemmerer, *Path to Freedom: The Struggle for Self-Government in Colonial New Jersey: 1703–1776* (Princeton: Princeton University Press, 1950), Chapters 10–11; McCormick, *New Jersey*, pp. 70–78; John E. Pomfret, *Colonial New Jersey: A History* (New York: Charles Scribner's Sons, 1973), pp. 153–166.

[17] Mark, *Agrarian Conflicts*, Chapters 4–5; Patricia U. Bonomi, *A Factious People: Politics and Society in Colonial New York* (New York: Columbia University Press, 1971), Chapter 6; Michael Kammen, *Colonial New York: A History* (New York: Charles Scribner's Sons, 1975), pp. 299–304; Countryman, "'Out of the Bounds of the Law'."

3. The Paxton Boys uprising in Pennsylvania, 1763–1764 [18]
4. The North Carolina Regulators of 1764–1771 [19]
5. The South Carolina Regulators of 1767–1769 [20]
6. The Green Mountain Boys' insurgency in Vermont, 1770–1775 [21]
7. The Shays Rebellion in Massachusetts, 1786–1787 [22]
8. The Whiskey Rebellion in southwest Pennsylvania, 1794 [23]
9. The Fries Rebellion in the Delaware River back country of Pennsylvania, 1799 [24]

[18] Brooke Hindle, "The March of the Paxton Boys," *William and Mary Quarterly*, 3rd ser., 3 (1946): 461–486; John R. Dunbar, ed., *The Paxton Papers* (The Hague: Martinus Nijhof, 1957); Wilbur R. Jacobs, ed., *The Paxton Riots and the Frontier Theory* (Chicago: Rand McNally, 1967); David Sloan, "Protest in Pre-Revolutionary America: The Paxton Example," *Indiana Social Studies Quarterly*, 27 (1974–75): 29–37. See, also, George W. Franz, "Paxton: A Study of Community Structure and Mobility in the Colonial Pennsylvania Backcountry" (Ph.D. dissertation, Rutgers University, 1975).

[19] Powell, Huhta, and Farnham, *Regulators in North Carolina*; John S. Bassett, "The Regulators of North Carolina (1765–1771)," American Historical Association, *Annual Report for the Year 1894*, pp. 141–212, remains the most comprehensive printed secondary account, but the most significant interpretation of the Regulators is to be found in two incisive, deeply researched articles by Marvin L. Michael Kay, "The Payment of Provincial and Local Taxes in North Carolina, 1748–1771," *William and Mary Quarterly*, 3rd ser., 26 (1969): 218–240, and "The North Carolina Regulation, 1766–1776: A Class Conflict," pp. 71–124, in Young, *American Revolution*. See, also, Hugh T. Lefler and William S. Powell, *Colonial North Carolina: A History* (New York: Charles Scribner's Sons, 1973), Chapter 10.

[20] Richard Maxwell Brown, *The South Carolina Regulators* (Cambridge: Harvard University Press, 1963); Hooker, *Carolina Backcountry*.

[21] Countryman, "'Out of the Bounds of the Law'"; Matt B. Jones, *Vermont in the Making, 1750–1777* (Cambridge: Harvard University Press, 1939), Chapter 13 and *passim*; Chilton Williamson, Sr., *Vermont in Quandary: 1763–1825* (Montpelier: Vermont Historical Society, 1949), pp. 10–36; Charles A. Jellison, *Ethan Allen: Frontier Rebel* (Syracuse: Syracuse University Press, 1969), Chapters 2–5; Mark, *Agrarian Conflicts*, Chapter 6.

[22] Marion L. Starkey, *A Little Rebellion* (New York: Alfred A. Knopf, 1955); Van Beck Hall, *Politics without Parties: Massachusetts, 1780–1791* (Pittsburgh: University of Pittsburgh Press, 1972), Chapter 7; Robert A. Feer, "Shays's Rebellion" (Ph.D. dissertation, Harvard University, 1958).

[23] Leland D. Baldwin, *Whiskey Rebels* (Pittsburgh: University of Pittsburgh Press, 1939).

[24] William W. H. Davis, *The Fries Rebellion: 1789–99* (Doylestown: Doylestown Publishing Co., 1899). Peter Levine, "The Fries Rebellion: Social Violence and the Politics of the New Nation," *Pennsylvania History*, 40 (1973): 241–258. Geographically, the nine back country rebellions of this study occurred in two northern and

Striking directly at the homestead ethic were the main grievances which activated these rebellions: land titles in jeopardy; oppressive taxes and debts; the activities of land speculators; and the threat by outlaws and Indians to the peaceful occupancy of the homestead. Not all grievances were felt equally—or at all—by all participants in the rebellious movements. In New Jersey, New York, and Vermont, the principal resentment stemmed from the threat to land titles and the related machinations of land speculators.[25] The taxation–debt factor was of prime importance in North Carolina whose back countrymen suffered under the heaviest taxation in the colonies;[26] in Massachusetts, where heavy taxes and foreclosures for insolvency were driving poor and medium-

---

southern sectors. Seven of them lay along a sweeping concave arc stretching from northern and western New England through New York and New Jersey to southwestern Pennsylvania. The remaining two rebellions were in the south, lying along a second concave arc extending from the northern North Carolina piedmont to western South Carolina. Thus, there was a notable gap in the middle of America, for back country rebellions were absent in Maryland and Virginia. Although the two Chesapeake commonwealths were not untouched by back country tumult, in neither case did it rise to the level of sustained rebellion. Maryland's boundary dispute with Pennsylvania was, at times from 1732 to 1736, a violent back country conflict but no more than that. During the Revolutionary War, Virginia had two particular movements in defense of the homestead ethic, but neither gained the status of rebellion. The first was an abortive uprising of tenants against the great planters of the Northern Neck in 1775. The second was a lynch-law movement against Tories and outlaws in southwest Virginia, 1779–1780, that later gained the endorsement of the state government. Edmund S. Morgan has, in effect, suggested a reason for the lack of back country rebellious activity in the Chesapeake region, 1740–1799: the creation of an eighteenth-century consensus among whites based on the exploitation of black labor through the large scale slavery system that had emerged by the early part of the century. Aubrey C. Land, *The Dulanys of Maryland* . . . (Baltimore: Johns Hopkins Press, 1968), pp. 141–145; Dale E. Benson, "Virginia: The Problem of Revolution and Social Control: (unpublished paper, Southern Historical Association, Washington, D.C., October 30, 1969), on the little known protest of the tenants; Richard Maxwell Brown, *Strain of Violence: Historical Studies of American Violence and Vigilantism* (New York: Oxford University Press, 1975), pp. 59–60, on the lynch-law movement; Edmund S. Morgan, *American Slavery, American Freedom: The Ordeal of Colonial Virginia* (New York: W. W. Norton, 1975).

25 Kemmerer, *Path to Freedom*, Chapter 10; Mark, *Agrarian Conflicts*, Chapters 4–5; Jellison, *Ethan Allen*, Chapter 2; Jones, *Vermont*, Chapters 8, 13; Countryman, " 'Out of the Bounds of the Law'," pp. 41–42.

26 Kay, "Payment of Provincial and Local Taxes."

sized farmers to the wall;[27] and in Pennsylvania in the 1790s when federal taxes on whiskey and property inspired rebellions.[28] In the cases of the Paxton Boys and the South Carolina Regulators, the principal cause of violent insurgency arose from the danger to the peaceful occupancy of the land. The Scotch–Irish and other frontiersmen of an extensive back country area around Paxton Township on the Susquehanna River recoiled against the brutal Indian depredations resulting from Pontiac's War in the summer and fall of 1763.[29] The pattern in South Carolina was similar, although the threat to the homestead ethic was different. There the danger by the middle and late 1760s came not from Indians but from rapacious outlaw gangs who plundered farms, tortured farmers, and kidnapped and violated their wives and daughters in the colonial period's worst crime wave.[30]

Out of these various grievances emerged the goals of the back country rebels. The goals differed from place to place but in sum there were four—all in response to the jeopardy to the homestead ethic: to secure land titles against interlopers; to trim the burden of debt and taxation on the small- and medium-scale farmers; to curb land speculators; and to guarantee the safety of the homestead in the face of Indian and outlaw attacks. Impelled by these grievances, motivated by these goals, the back country rebels attacked three categories of enemies. In particular, there were two contrasting elites whom the back countrymen opposed with word and deed. One was an outside establishment of political and economic grandees who sought to dominate the back country to the disadvantage of the settlers. The other was an internal back country establishment that was either hostile or indifferent to the welfare of the rebels. The back countrymen were seldom able to inflict violence on the elite outsiders whom they attacked more characteristically with sizzling pamphlets or petitions.[31] More vul-

---

27 Starkey, *Little Rebellion*, pp. 14–17; Hall, *Politics without Parties*, pp. 189–194.
28 Baldwin, *Whiskey Rebels*; Levine, "Fries Rebellion."
29 Dunbar, *Paxton Papers*, pp. 16–21, 185–186, 295.
30 Brown, *South Carolina Regulators*, pp. 27–37.
31 Numerous examples include Husband, *Impartial Relation*; the Paxton Boys' *Declaration and Remonstrance*, 1764, reprinted in Dunbar, *Paxton Papers*, pp. 99–110; and the South Carolina Regulators' remonstrance, November, 1767, printed in Hooker, *Carolina Backcountry*, pp. 213–246.

nerable to the violence of the rebels were the internal back country establishments and, especially, the back country clients of the outside and inside elites. These back country dependents of wealthier men were often competing settlers who invoked land titles, supported by the outsiders, in an attempt to displace the pioneers who were to be found in the rebel ranks.

In New Jersey the hostile outside elite was, collectively, the East Jersey Proprietors—a narrow body of landed magnates headed by the New Jersey chief justice, Robert Hunter Morris, and the eminent attorney, James Alexander.[32] The East Jersey Proprietors claimed title to great stretches of land in northern and western New Jersey. The proprietors aggressively attempted to collect quitrents (that is, land taxes) from those already settled on the land or to oust recalcitrant settlers in favor of those who would acknowledge the original land ownership of the Proprietors and pay the quitrents.[33] Pennsylvania of the 1760s found the Paxtonites and other back countrymen confronting a hated outside elite, the Quaker mercantile aristocracy of Philadelphia that generally dominated the colony's legislature. The Quaker establishment, so the Paxton Boys charged, refused to vote adequate funds and measures for frontier defense against the Indians. Such inaction came not only from Quaker principles of pacifism but also, the back country dissidents felt, from crass indifference to the safety of the frontier.[34] To the Green Mountain Boys, the external enemy was a clique of New York land speculators headed by James Duane, John Reid, and John Kempe—men who claimed, by virtue of the broader pretensions of New York colony, to hold title to the lands settled by the Green Mountain Boys who, in turn, traced their titles to earlier grants made by New Hampshire.[35] In Massachusetts, those who followed Daniel Shays and called themselves "Regulators" in emulation of the earlier uprisings in North and South Carolina found their supreme oppressors in a state government dominated by the commercially oriented cities of eastern

32 Kemmerer, *Path to Freedom*, Chapter 10.
33 Ibid.
34 Dunbar, *Paxton Papers*, p. 271 and *passim*; Hindle, "March of the Paxton Boys," pp. 463–464; Sloan, "Protest," pp. 30–32.
35 Jellison, *Ethan Allen*, pp. 36–38, 50, 80–81.

Massachusetts and especially by urban interests in Boston.[36] The objects of back country animus in both the Whiskey and Fries Rebellions of Pennsylvania were the Federalist Party administrations in the national capital who imposed the detested new taxes on whiskey and land.[37] In two other cases, there were outside establishments that provoked the secondary resentment of the back country rebels. These were, in South Carolina, the Low Country elite of great planters, merchants, and lawyers, and, in North Carolina, a provincewide establishment, centered in the eastern coastal plain, that dominated the colony's assembly.[38]

Internal to the back country were the affiliates of the outside elites. Among these dependent back country clienteles were the Conestoga Indians of Pennsylvania who, domiciled peaceably within the frontier settlements, drew the full force of the wrath of the pioneers who had suffered piteously from the onslaughts of the warring tribes in 1763.[39] In New Jersey there were the Proprietary grantees who disputed the land titles of the rioters,[40] while in New York there were the docile lessees of the great Hudson River landlords who would have displaced the rural rebels of the back country.[41] Opposing the Green Mountain Boys were the New York sponsored settlers of such Vermont communities as Panton and Clarendon who in increasing numbers would have crowded the insurgents off the land.[42] South Carolina's back country had a polygot mixture of outlaws and "lower people" whom the Regulators claimed were linked not with the outside Low Country elite but with certain leading men of the back country itself.[43] The back country rebels waged war on these elements among them, in actions ranging from the massacre of the Conestogas to various physical assaults and house burnings in the other cases.

[36] Hall, *Politics without Parties*, Chapter 1.

[37] Baldwin, *Whiskey Rebels*; Davis, *Fries Rebellion*, pp. 109–110 and *passim*.

[38] Brown, *South Carolina Regulators*, pp. 42–43 and *passim*; Kay, "North Carolina Regulation," p. 77; Lefler and Powell, *Colonial North Carolina*, Chapter 10.

[39] Dunbar, *Paxton Papers*, pp. 23–28; Hindle, "March of the Paxton Boys," p. 467, notes that some of the Conestogas, individually, had maintained contact with the hostile Indians.

[40] Countryman, " 'Out of the Bounds of the Law'," pp. 39, 45.

[41] Mark, *Agrarian Conflicts*, pp. 122–129.

[42] Jellison, *Ethan Allen*, pp. 80, 86–89; Jones, *Vermont*, pp. 303–307, 322–326.

[43] Brown, *South Carolina Regulators*, pp. 84–88.

The dependent back countrymen whom the rebels attacked were generally of the same lower and middle social stature as the rebels themselves, but this was not true of the internal back country elites who attracted the hatred and sometimes the violence of the insurgents. Unlike the mass of the rebels, the detested back country elites were positioned at the upper level of the social structure and formed, as it were, the back country establishments. Of all the antirebel back country elites, the most glittering and powerful were the great landlords of the east shore of the Hudson in New York—the families of Livingstons, Van Rensselaers, Philipses, Cortlandts, and others. Too well protected to suffer personal injury at the hands of the antirent rioters, the landlords were, rather, the targets of intermittent guerrilla warfare against their properties and dependents in a campaign that came to a peak in 1766.[44] Enjoying something of the same protected status in New Jersey were the likes of county judge Samuel Neville who strongly supported the East Jersey Proprietors against the land rioters.[45] More vulnerable were the back country establishments elsewhere—especially in North Carolina where the local elites of county judges, officials, and lawyers were the most rapacious, oppressive, and greedy of all the elites inside or outside the back country. Nor did the North Carolina Regulators scruple to attack the persons and properties of such despised members of the back country elite as Judge Richard Henderson and attorneys Edmund Fanning and John Williams.[46] The Green Mountain Boys were similarly severe with members of the pro-New York internal elite.[47] The Regulators who enlisted in the Massachusetts movement headed by Daniel Shays and others took aim at the county judges and the high-toned residents of the scattering of commercial centers, such as Springfield, that were found here and there in

---

[44] Mark, *Agrarian Conflicts*, Chapter 5.

[45] Countryman, "'Out of the Bounds of the Law'," p. 43; Pomfret, *Colonial New Jersey*, p. 153.

[46] Bassett, "Regulators," pp. 188–189.

[47] Mark, *Agrarian Conflicts*, pp. 181, 185, 188–189; Jones, *Vermont*, pp. 292–293, 325–326, 333–335. Jellison, *Ethan Allen*, pp. 63–66, 86–89. Among those attacked were magistrates John Munro and Benjamin Spencer and the Reverend Benjamin Hough.

the back country.[48] In the Pennsylvania of the 1790s, it was the local Federalist officialdom and their supporters who felt the anger of the antitax rebels in the Whiskey and Fries uprisings.[49]

IV. Patterns of Leadership

In the realm of leadership, organization, and actions, particular patterns emerge just as they do in respect to grievances, goals, and targets. The nine back country rebellions were sustained uprisings that, in most cases, lasted a year or more and, in several cases, for many years.[50] Frequently growing out of the prerebellion organizational structure of the back country—particularly the militia—the insurgent movements were often carefully organized. The framework of the typical rebellion was generally military or quasi-military in character. In some cases—most notably in New Jersey, New York, and South Carolina—the military arms of the rebellion simply usurped the status of the regular militia companies.[51] While the organization of most of the back country rebellions is impressive, the greater distinctiveness of these uprisings is found in the character of their remarkable leadership. Normally the popular movements of American history—whether violent or nonviolent—have drawn their leaders from the social aristocracy as examples as diverse as Nathaniel Bacon, Thomas Jefferson, and Franklin D. Roosevelt indicate. Yet, the opposite was the case with the nine back country rebellions whose leaders were socially endogenous.

Thus, the protagonists of the back country rebellions rose

[48] Hall, *Politics without Parties*, pp. 204–205; Starkey, *Little Rebellion*, pp. 30–31 and *passim*.

[49] Davis, *Fries Rebellion*, pp. 6, 40. Individuals singled out for attack included John Neville by the Whiskey rebels and by the Fries rebels federal marshal William Nichols and federal tax assessors James Chapman, John Rodrock, and Everhard Foulke.

[50] Lengths of movements: 15 years—N. J. land rioters; 14 years—N. Y. antirenters; 8 years—North Carolina Regulators; 6 years—Green Mountain Boys; 2 years—South Carolina Regulators; 7 months—Shays Rebellion; 5 months—Whiskey Rebellion; 3 months—Paxton Boys and Fries Rebellion.

[51] Countryman, " 'Out of the Bounds of the Law'," pp. 42–43; Brown, *South Carolina Regulators*, pp. 56–57.

from the people but, unlike John Adams of the patriot movement, for example, did not rise above them. The back country rebel leaders stood no higher in the social order than the agrarian middle class; they were men of medium property and landholdings. Coming out of obscurity, these rebel chiefs stepped to the fore in the van of the popular uprisings, but once the rebellions ended most of them faded back into the shadows from which they had emerged.[52] One such leader was Seth Warner of the Green Mountain Boys. Less well known today than the colorful Ethan Allen, Warner, concedes Allen's biographer, "towered head and shoulders among all others including Ethan Allen himself." The dynamic Allen with his spectacular exploits and incisive writings was bound to eclipse the reputations of less glamorous but more solid leaders such as Warner, Remember Baker, Thomas Chittenden, and Robert Cochran. Warner, not Allen, was in the first wave of Connecticut migrants to Vermont, and it was Warner, not Allen, who spearheaded a "paramilitary protective association" of Bennington farmers against the New York land claimants. In his humble, untutored origins, Warner was typical of the back country rebel leaders, for in his youth he had been better known for "his skill in woodcraft than his acquaintance with books." He grew into "a big man of great bodily strength and majestic appearance" who came to be a more admired leader of the Green Mountain Boys than the flashier Allen. Warner completely eschewed the small-scale land speculating activities that attracted Ethan Allen and lived out his Vermont days in an unpretentious hillside farm house.[53]

[52] Ethan Allen is the obvious exception to the generalization. Yet, Allen is closer to the prototype of the obscure back country leader than to the characteristically upwardly mobile revolutionary leader dealt with by Elkins and McKitrick (see below at note 61). Edward Countryman, " 'Out of the Bounds of the Law'," p. 53, correctly notes that the Onion River Land Co. headed by Allen was a combine of "petty speculators at most." When Allen died in 1789, he and his young wife had been living well but far from luxuriously in a Bennington rooming house. Owning about 12,000 acres at death, Allen was, however, land poor; he had little cash and in 1786 had narrowly escaped a term in the debtors' prison. Jellison, *Ethan Allen*, pp. 320–322. On John Adams, see Robert Zemsky, *Merchants, Farmers, and River Gods* (Boston: Gambit, 1971) .

[53] Jellison, *Ethan Allen*, pp. 40–41; "Warner, Seth," *Dictionary of American Biography, s. v.*

The names of Daniel Shays and John Fries still resound through history in so far as their names have been attached to movements they led, but each man was distinctly small time. Before appearing at the head of the back country Regulator movement in Massachusetts, Shays had been an honorable but unremarked junior officer in the Revolutionary War. After the Revolution, Shays gained no higher distinction than town official in the back country village of Pelham. Nor did Shays do any better after the rebellion of 1786–1787, for, following his pardon, he merely moved farther into the back country in western New York.[54] Even more obscure was John Fries, whose attainments were no higher than that of rural auctioneer and minor militia officer. But among his avid rebel following, Fries's lack of high social standing was outweighed by the flair of his personality. Hotly opposed to oppression of all sorts, he was "an easy and fluent talker" with "a species of rude eloquence which gave him a great control over the multitude."[55] For all their audacity, Amos Roberts and William Prendergast, the indomitable protagonists of the New Jersey and New York uprisings, respectively, were no more than common farmers. Yet, by his followers Roberts "was reverenced as much as if he had been a king."[56] Prendergast, who in 1766 defied all the legal and armed might of the province of New York, was likewise a hero to his followers. They viewed him as "a sober, honest, and industrious Farmer much beloved by his neighbors" of Dutchess County—one who took up the cause of the antirenters because "he pitied poor people who were turned out of possession" of their land by the great landlords.[57]

<hr/>

[54] "Shays, John," *Dictionary of American Biography, s. v.* Other leaders of the Massachusetts Regulators included Luke Day and Adam Wheeler. They and the persons cited below in notes 55 and 57–60 conformed to the back country rebel leader prototype sketched here.

[55] Davis, *Fries Rebellion,* pp. 8–11; "Fries, John," *Dictionary of American Biography, s. v.* Other leaders of the rebellion included John Getman and Fred Heany.

[56] Kemmerer, *Path to Freedom,* pp. 217–218.

[57] Mark, *Agrarian Conflicts,* p. 146; Irving Mark and Oscar Handlin, eds., "Land Causes in Colonial New York, 1765–1767: The King v. William Prendergast," *New York University Law Quarterly Review,* 19 (1941–42): 165–194. Other antirent rebel leaders included Michael Hallenbeck and Samuel Munroe.

These men all had the status of folk leaders as did Thomas Woodward, the Regulator, in South Carolina. In his back country neighborhood along Little River and Cedar Creek in present Fairfield County, Woodward was "a terror" to the "evil-doers" who precipitated the Regulator movement by their outlaw activities. As a frontier planter, Woodward stood out among the Regulators by virtue, not of excessive wealth, for that he lacked, but of his commanding presence. "Possessing strong but agreeable features" and being "considerably over common size," Woodward remained a personal rallying point for his neighbors who gathered in defense of the homestead even after the Regulators had repulsed the outlaw threat: Before his death in 1779 Woodward, in the early years of the Revolution, "aided efficiently in keeping . . . in check" the local Tories whose "dry bones . . . shook at the very name of Woodward."[58] A bluff personal style comparable to that of Woodward characterized the roving frontiersman and Paxtonite leader, Captain Lazarus Stewart. After serving in the fore of the Paxton movement, Stewart and some of his followers moved in 1769 to another Pennsylvania back country trouble spot, the Wyoming Valley. There his successful leadership of the Connecticut immigrants and their Pennsylvania allies in the Yankee–Pennamite turbulence, 1769–1775, replicated his Paxton career.[59]

Of all the endogenous leaders of the back country rebellions, the most intriguing was Hermon Husband who turned up as a member of not just one but two of these movements—first, the North Carolina Regulators, and then, very late in life, the Whiskey Rebellion. Husband was a peripatetic pioneer who moved about from his Maryland birthplace to the North Carolina piedmont, back to Maryland after the shattering of the Regulator uprising, and, finally, to the far western frontier of Pennsylvania. Deeply affected in his youth by the Great Awakening, Husband combined religious pacifism which prevented him from taking part in the

[58] Brown, *South Carolina Regulators*, pp. 130–132.   An extended biographical sketch of Woodward will appear in Richard Maxwell Brown, *Prosopography of the South Carolina Regulators* (University of South Carolina Press, forthcoming) . Other South Carolina Regulator leaders included Barnaby Pope and Gideon Gibson.

[59] Dunbar, *Paxton Papers*, p. 24; Hindle, "March of the Paxton Boys," pp. 485–486; "Stewart, Lazarus," *Dictionary of American Biography*, s. v. Other leaders of the Paxton Boys were Matthew Smith and James Gibson.

violence of either the Regulator or the Whiskey Rebel movements with a strongly felt, self-taught indoctrination in libertarian ideas that put him at the head of the Regulator movement as both an eloquent speaker—"a firebrand amongst the people"—and a skilled pamphleteer. Yet, Husband, for all his talent as a writer and an ideologue and his intellectual sophistication that was far above that of the average leader of the back country rebellions, was never able to become more—and perhaps never aspired for more—on the material side of life than a successful back country farmer.[60]

Many years ago, Stanley Elkins and Eric McKitrick published a seminal article on the "young men of the Revolution" in which they ably made the point that the most eminent founding fathers combined upward social mobility with patriotic leadership.[61] More recently, and with exhaustive quantitative evidence, James K. Martin has viewed the Revolution as an event which significantly expanded the office-holding status of members of the local elites.[62] In striking contrast was the role of the leaders of the back country rebellions who, for the most part, demonstrated neither upward social nor political mobility. Except for Allen, Warner, and Baker of the Green Mountain Boys, these men did not ascend into the provincial or state levels of political power. Nor did they improve their personal property to any striking degree, if at all; and here the Green Mountain leaders do not form an exception to the rule.[63] The back country rebel leaders lacked the social and economic background, the education, the subtlety, and, quite

[60] Mary E. Lazenby, *Herman Husband: A Story of His Life* (Washington, D.C.: Old Neighborhood Press, 1940). Powell, Huhta, and Farnham, *Regulators in North Carolina*, pp. 222–238, 300–303, 568–569; "Husbands [*sic*], Hermon," *Dictionary of American Biography, s. v;* Alan Heimert and Perry Miller, eds., *The Great Awakening* (Indianapolis: Bobbs-Merrill, 1967), pp. 636–654. Other North Carolina Regulator leaders were Rednap Howell (the movement's song writer), William Butler, and Samuel Devinney.

[61] Stanley Elkins and Eric McKitrick, "The Founding Fathers: Young Men of the Revolution," *Political Science Quarterly*, 76 (1961): 181–216.

[62] James K. Martin, *Men in Rebellion: Higher Governmental Leaders and the Coming of the American Revolution* (New Brunswick: Rutgers University Press, 1973).

[63] Warner and Allen are discussed, above, at note 53. On Baker: "Baker, Remember," *Dictionary of American Biography, s. v.*

possibly, the ambition to rise to higher levels of social status and political leadership.[64] They were true popular leaders in that they never outgrew the common element of their inelegant social origins. In one way, this was a source of strength for these popular rebellions. Endogenous leaders like Husband, Warner, Woodward, Roberts, Prendergast, and the others had the unambivalent trust and devotion of their adherents. There was no social distance between leaders and followers to breed mistrust and cynicism on the part of either.

Lacking social distinction, these men of the people possessed instead a personal charisma which made them remarkable leaders of unremarkable individuals. Fully matched to their followers in terms of class and status, the endogenous rebel chieftains were limited men—limited not merely in wealth or official rank but in the even more crucial categories of personal aspiration, social horizon, and political objective. Here was a notable weakness of the back country rebellions, for, popular in character and standing for the protodemocratic values of the homestead ethic, it must be emphasized that, except for the Green Mountain Boys, they never advanced beyond a subcolony or substate regional base. This was caused partly by the limited character of their leaders.

V. Patterns of Activity

The restricted nature of the back country rebellions is apparent not only in their leadership but in their actions, which were bound by the landscape as well as the ideology of the homestead. Thus, most of the activity of the rebels took place in the back country locales where the homestead was culturally and ethically dominant. Like their urban counterparts in the riotous city mobs of the revolutionary era, the back country rebels killed few of their victims. The only significant departure from this

---

[64] The back country rebel leaders are to be compared to the prototypical backward Americans of the eighteenth century discussed by James Henretta in "The Quantification of Consciousness" (unpublished paper, Conference on Early American Social History, State University of New York at Stony Brook, June 1975).

characteristic was the case of the Paxton Boys who slaughtered a remnant of the Conestoga Indians of the Pennsylvania back country.[65] Much more common than killing was corporal punishment—the sometimes vicious beating or flogging of individuals—that was the favorite sanction, along with arson, of the back country rebels.[66] Transcending the ubiquitous episodes of corporal punishment and arson was the even more significant vendetta against regular law enforcement: against the local, regional, or external agents of the law—the judges who laid it down, the sheriffs and others who enforced it, the jailers who sequestered those who broke it, and the lawyers who exploited it for their own devious ends. Prototypically antilegal were the South Carolina Regulators who stopped the judicial processes of the province of South Carolina in the back country, and, in precedent-setting vigilante fashion, took the law into their own hands against the bandits and ne'er-do-wells in their midst. Nor did the Regulators hesitate to free their own members who had been taken into custody by provincial officers determined to break up their rampant vigilantism.[67]

All but one of the remaining eight back country rebellions exemplified the antilegal norm of the South Carolina Regulators. The New Jersey land rioters blatantly defied judicial actions in favor of the East Jersey Proprietors, and the former regularly broke into jails to free those who had been imprisoned for opposing the Proprietors.[68] In similar fashion, the New York antirent rebels rescued men from the custody of the law.[69] In analogy to South Carolina's Regulators who thwarted the Low Country–dominated courts in that colony, the Green Mountain Boys would not allow courts with an external sponsorship—that of New York

---

[65] Dunbar, *Paxton Papers*, pp. 23–24, 28.

[66] Brown, *South Carolina Regulators*, pp. 38–41, 46, 49–50, 89–91. The Regulators hanged 16 outlaws, but this was in a ranger campaign authorized by the provincial government. See also Countryman, " 'Out of the Bounds of the Law'," p. 39 and *passim*.

[67] Brown, *South Carolina Regulators*, Chapters 3–4.

[68] Kemmerer, *Path to Freedom*, Chapter 10.

[69] Mark, *Agrarian Conflicts*, p. 140 and *passim*.

—to sit in the present Vermont area.[70] The ire of the North Carolina Regulators was directed most of all at the county courthouse rings—the clusters of judges, officials, and attorneys who, with slanted decisions, outrageous fees, spurious seizures of property for taxes or debt, and prejudicial pleadings, oppressed the back country small- and medium-size farmers until at last they arose in the Regulator movement and drove judges from the bench, threatened officials, whipped obnoxious lawyers, and rioted in the county seats.[71] The back country throngs of Massachusetts men who eventually fell in behind Daniel Shays called themselves "Regulators," because, following the pattern of their namesakes in North and South Carolina, they wished to regulate the courts—as they put it—by preventing the county courts of common pleas from sitting. The Massachusetts Regulators, during the summer and fall of 1786, did intimidate the common pleas courts into adjournment. This saved the landholdings of many back country farmers who, in the grips of depression and a regressive tax system, could pay neither debts nor taxes and thus stood to lose their properties.[72] In southwestern Pennsylvania, the Whiskey Rebels sought to stop the collection of the excise on whiskey by moving against the federal inspectors and marshals who enforced the tax law, a course replicated by the militant followers of John Fries 5 years later as they poured scalding hot water on some federal tax assessors and captured others as well as forcibly freeing arrested tax resisters from the Bethlehem jail.[73]

Typically, the South Carolina Regulators successfully sealed off the back country from the outside interference of the courts and officials based in the Low Country metropolis of Charleston.[74] With the lone exception of the Paxton Boys, the other back country rebel movements resembled the South Carolina Regula-

[70] Ibid., p. 177.

[71] Powell, *Regulators in North Carolina*, pp. 24–25; Kay, "North Carolina Regulation," p. 98.

[72] Starkey, *Little Rebellion*, pp. 14, 17–18, 26, 30–39, 57–59, 61–62.

[73] Baldwin, *Whiskey Rebels*; Levine, "Fries Rebellion."

[74] Brown, *South Carolina Regulators*, pp. 53–60.

tors in their attempts to block off their localities from outside interference—to take control of their homestead areas from antagonistic courts and officials. This strategy was audacious in its defiance of colony, state, and federal governments, but it was limited in scope and essentially defensive in character. In eight of the nine insurgent movements, offensive operations were not undertaken away from the back country regional base. Only the Paxton Boys marched to their provincial capital,[75] and, as noted, the Paxtonites were the single exception to the rebel thrust against courts and officials. The New York antirenters and the South Carolina Regulators threatened to march into their respective capitals but wisely never did so.[76] The North and South Carolina Regulators raised sizable military detachments, but they were aligned primarily for defense of their back country strongholds rather than for sorties outward.[77] The defensive instinct of the back country rebels was sound, for the North Carolina Regulator movement was overwhelmed by an invasion of North Carolina militia under the command of Governor William Tryon at the back country battle of Alamance in 1771, and earlier, in 1766, a comparable force of militia and royal troops suppressed the New York antirenters.[78] Outland detachments were also mainly responsible for the defeat of the Shays, Whiskey, and Fries rebels. The quarantining and defense of the back country regions by the various rebel movements demonstrated both the depth of feeling behind the homestead ethic and the limitations of that emotion. In effect, the back country insurgents would not go beyond the local realm of the homestead to advance the causes for which they rose. The back country rebels of 1740–1799 were, thus, socially more radical but politically less radical than the revolutionary patriots of 1776. The back countrymen wished only to defend themselves and their homesteads against the manifold forces that endangered them. Unlike the revolutionary patriots, they sought

---

[75] Hindle, "March of the Paxton Boys."

[76] Bonomi, *Factious People*, p. 180; Brown, *South Carolina Regulators*, p. 61.

[77] Kay, "North Carolina Regulation," pp. 90, 101–102; Brown, *South Carolina Regulators*, p. 94.

[78] Kay, "North Carolina Regulation," pp. 100–103; Mark, *Agrarian Conflicts*, pp. 147–149.

94

not to overturn the structure of government but only to make it more socially responsive to their grievances.[79]

VI. Conclusions

In conclusion, there are two questions to consider: First, what was the outcome of the nine back country rebellions? Second, why were the rebellions at an end by 1800? Why, indeed, were they on the wane by the 1780s? The image of the rebellions is one of failure—in no small part due to the ignominious military defeats of the North Carolina Regulators at Alamance in 1771 and of the Massachusetts Shaysites at Springfield and Petersham in early 1787. Well known, too, is the inglorious end of the Whiskey Rebellion as the insurgents simply melted away in the face of the imposing federal army sent into the back country.

Yet, the image of failure is deceptive, for, on closer examination, the rebellions were far more successful than the image suggests. The box score for all nine movements reveals that complete triumphs in the de jure as well as de facto sense were scored by the South Carolina Regulators and the Green Mountain Boys. De facto victories were the achievement of the New Jersey land rioters, who repelled the East Jersey Proprietors to the extent that the latter simply gave up after almost two decades of trying to conquer the insurgents, and of the Paxton Boys, who not only successfully defied the provincial government but, as James H. Hutson has maintained, precipitated a significant reorientation of Pennsylvania politics in the late colonial period.[80] Hence, four of the nine rebellions were clearly successful. Two more were unmitigated failures in the short term but not in the long run. Thus, the Shays Regulators were sharply defeated on the battlefield, but their supporters were so numerous in the back country

---

[79] See, for example, Sloan, "Protest," pp. 30, 34.

[80] Brown, *South Carolina Regulators*, Chapters 6–7; Mark, *Agrarian Conflicts*, pp. 197–199; James H. Hutson, *Pennsylvania Politics, 1746–1770: The Movement for Royal Government and Its Consequences* (Princeton: Princeton University Press, 1972), pp. 120–121.

and the state as a whole that, following the suppression of the rebellion, their political opponents in the faction led by Governor James Bowdoin were stunningly defeated in the Massachusetts election of 1787. In effect, Shays and his men won back at the polls what they lost in the field, a reversal so abrupt that Van Beck Hall, the leading authority, ironically characterized the election result as "the revolution of 1787." [81]

Political success in the aftermath of military defeat is less evident in the cases of New York in 1766 and North Carolina in 1771, but mild reform in response to rebel grievances outlasted the immediate reprisals against the land rioters and Regulators, respectively.[82] An even longer range viewpoint is needed to put the Whiskey and Fries rebellions in perspective. Each rebellion was easily crushed by the armed might of the national government, but, insofar as the animus of both movements was against the Federalist Party, whose tax legislation provoked their uprisings, it is worth noting that the national political ascendancy of the Federalists was at an end within 2 years of the suppression of the Fries Rebellion. Although national governmental power was most significantly the winner in both the Whiskey and Fries episodes, the fate of the Federalist Party was actually the same as the two rebellions; it simply died a slower and more agonizing death. The anti-Federalist sentiment expressed violently in the Whiskey and Fries rebellions of the 1790s became the reigning American public opinion after 1800.

In general, then, the back country rebellions, 1740 to 1799, were largely successful. Yet, the final question remains: Why had the rebellions faded away by the early 1800s? The answer is to be found in two emergent and converging trends of the late eighteenth century. One trend was the gradual alleviation of the land–population–wealth crisis, as the population pressure on the land was significantly relieved by the post–Revolutionary War advance of settlement into the vast area west of the Appalachians.[83]

[81] Hall, *Politics without Parties*, Chapter 8.

[82] Mark, *Agrarian Conflicts*, p. 202; Kay, "North Carolina Regulation," pp. 99, 104.

[83] Ray Allen Billington, *Westward Expansion: A History of the American Frontier*, 3rd ed. (New York: Macmillan, 1967), Chapters 12, 14–15.

Dramatically but not untypically illustrating the waning of the land–population–wealth crisis was the career of Andrew Jackson. As James C. Curtis emphasizes in his recent biographical study of Old Hickory, there was much too little potential for economic and social advancement in the constricted and conflict-ridden South Carolina–North Carolina back country where Jackson passed his restless youth. With prospects so discouraging in the old Regulator regions, the still young Andrew set out for Tennessee where he soon rocketed from the obscurity of his origins in the Carolina back country to the top of the heap in the booming Nashville area.[84]

The second trend accounting for the decline of the back country rebellions was the shift of their main thrust from violence to political action. This was a gradual process of long duration whose origins, and no more, may be perceived in the 1770s and 1780s. The rebellions had occurred because the ordinary peaceful political means of conflict resolution had proved to be inadequate. But, insofar as the overall objective of the back country rebellions was the defense of land and life in the interest of the homestead ethic, a political outlet of reform rather than rebellion opened toward the end of the eighteenth century. In that era, as the colonial period of the 1760s and 1770s merged into the national period of the 1770s and 1780s, a new threat to the homestead ideal arose. It was far more dangerous in its potential than were the localized threats that precipitated the nine back country rebellions. The new development was a danger national in scope. It stemmed from the giant land speculation syndicates organized in the 1760s and 1770s whose goal, cumulatively, was no less than the engrossing of virtually all of the land in the huge belt of unsettled territory stretching from present West Virginia and Tennessee to the Great Lakes and the Mississippi River. Spearheading this unprecedented movement of speculative enterprise was the pervasive Anglo-American cartel headed by London banker and politico,

---

[84] James C. Curtis, *Andrew Jackson and the Search for Vindication* (Boston: Little, Brown, 1976), Chapters 1–2. See also Michael Paul Rogin, *Fathers and Children: Andrew Jackson and the Subjugation of the American Indian* (New York: Alfred A. Knopf, 1975), Chapter 2.

Thomas Walpole, and including, eventually, such Americans as
Samuel Wharton, Benjamin Franklin, and Robert Morris.[85]

Land speculation did occur in the Old Northwest and the
Old Southwest, but, to abridge a long, tangled tale, it did so on a
far smaller scale than was envisioned by Thomas Walpole and his
American associates. With its powerful adherents on both sides of
the Atlantic, the Walpole scheme transcended the divisions of
revolution and war to persist on into the 1780s. That it was ultimately defeated was attributable in no small degree to Thomas
Jefferson who provided a philosophical viewpoint as well as a
tactical gambit in opposition to the super land speculators. It was
Jefferson's idea, expressed as early as 1774 but repeated strikingly
in 1776 and thereafter, that every settler was entitled to the free
grant of a family-size farm in the great West—what would in the
nineteenth century be specifically termed a homestead.[86] Symbol-
izing Jefferson's allegiance to the homestead ethic was his famous
advocacy of the measures abolishing primogeniture and entail in
Virginia. More to the point, however, in defending the homestead
ideal and much more practical in impact was a Virginia law of
1779 cosponsored by Jefferson and George Mason. This was a
pre-emption law, the first of its kind passed by an American
legislature—one that would be followed in 10 years by the passage
of similar laws in North Carolina and Pennsylvania where back
country rebellious activity was strong.[87] Not for several decades
did the campaign for a national pre-emption law gain success, but

[85] Thomas P. Abernethy, *Western Lands and the American Revolution* (New
York: D. Appleton-Century, 1937), pp. 45, 216, 285, and *passim*; Jack M. Sosin, *The
Revolutionary Frontier, 1763–1783* (New York: Holt, Rinehart and Winston, 1967),
pp. 33, 36, and *passim*; Richard B. Morris, *The Peacemakers: The Great Powers
and American Independence* (New York: Harper and Row, 1965), p. 249 and
passim.

[86] Thomas Jefferson, *A Summary View of the Rights of British America* . . .
(Williamsburg: Clementina Rind, 1774); Julian P. Boyd, ed., *The Papers of
Thomas Jefferson* (Princeton: Princeton University Press, 1950), vol. 1, pp. 362,
492; vol. 2, p. 140; Dumas Malone, *Jefferson the Virginian* (Boston: Little, Brown,
1948), pp. 251–252; Merrill D. Peterson, *Thomas Jefferson and the New Nation:
A Biography* (New York: Oxford University Press, 1970), pp. 113–124.

[87] Boyd, *Papers of Thomas Jefferson*, vol. 2, pp. 155–157; Malone, *Jefferson the
Virginian*, pp. 258–259; Amelia C. Ford, *Colonial Precedents of our National Land
System as It Existed in 1800* (Madison: University of Wisconsin, 1910), pp. 127–134.

the movement for the pre-emption law evolved naturally into the more advanced drive for the Homestead Act signed into law by Abraham Lincoln.[88] Jefferson and his progressive colleagues in Virginia had subtly initiated a shift by the protagonists of the homestead ethic from the course of violent rebellion of 1740–1799 to the nonviolent political activity in behalf of the agrarian objectives of pre-emption, land prices graduated downward, and, ultimately, free land.

[88] Roy M. Robbins, *Our Landed Heritage: The Public Domain, 1776–1936* (Lincoln: University of Nebraska Press, 1962), pp. 10–11, 19, 30–31, 48–50; Don E. Fehrenbacher, *The Era of Expansion, 1800–1848* (New York: John Wiley and Sons, 1968), pp. 40–43.

III

THE PERSPECTIVE
OF MODERNIZATION

5

The American Revolution, Modernization, and Man: A Critique

Kenneth A. Lockridge

In an article on the American Revolution published in 1973, I expressed skepticism concerning the word *modernization* as applied to colonial and revolutionary America. Instead I perceived a more limited, complex, contradictory, and inadvertent sociopolitical process, one that altered men's interests, provoked defensive responses, and "modernized" perhaps a few men, but whose "modernizing" influence was chiefly viable in the creation of a political framework that enabled the nation–state to accommodate the multiplying interests of a diverse society. In general, I posited no restructuring of human relationships or of the human psyche, but principally only of interests and their interaction, expression, and means of accommodation.[1]

Lately I have become even more skeptical about modernization in this and in later contexts. True, Western historians have extended the process of modernization in the West over a vast

[1] Kenneth A. Lockridge, "Social Change and the Meaning of the American Revolution," *Journal of Social History*, 6 (1973): 403–439.

span of time, making it more subtle in the process. They now speak of a long stage of attitudinal preparation for modernization lasting from perhaps 1500 to 1850. Yet even this initial stage is still seen as a process whose chief product was presumably a self-conscious, rational, calculating, choice-making, planning, manipulative individual. The shaping of this individual was to some degree a precondition for the subsequent stages of urbanization and industrialization which utterly modernized society, in its external aspect, and presumably altered men still further internally.[2] Thus historians still tend to regard even the first stage of Western modernization as a more total transformation of human relations and of the human psyche than I find consistent with the evidence. I am not so sure about the later stages either. It seems possible that the human personality has changed less than the literature on modernization would have us believe.

I. Modernization and the Revolution

Let me once again use the literature on the American Revolution as a point of departure in expressing this enhanced skepticism. There has arisen in recent years an immense literature which speaks in terms of the progressive social modernization of colonial Americans and speaks above all of the boost given this modernization by the processes of the Revolution itself. This literature concentrates mostly on the years during and after the Revolution and emphasizes the nearly total modernization of the American individual and so of American society. What I propose to do is to present this literature in its widest and most persuasive aspect, then comment upon the view of modernization implicit in the works of Charles Tilly. My point is that I am both sympathetic to and skeptical about this growing emphasis on modernization in the America of 1750–1830, and that I would like to develop a more limited way of viewing the vast social changes experienced by Western man.

[2] See, for example, E. A. Wrigley, "The Process of Modernization and the Industrial Revolution in England," *Journal of Interdisciplinary History*, 3 (1972–73): 225–259.

The essential feature of this new literature on early American society and the American Revolution is its insistence, implicit or explicit, on the ultimate production of a "new man" very like "modern man" as defined by Professor Alex Inkeles.[3] This man is the opposite of traditional, collective, localistic, and fatalistic; he is modern, individualistic, cosmopolitan, active, and optimistic. The literature speaks in terms of the innately liberating effects of the raw American environment and then shifts to the increasing degree of geographic and social mobility and social diversity and choice in eighteenth-century America. In crudest form, the result is John A. Garraty's new man, facing westward, Bernard Bailyn's "typical American optimism, individualism, and enterprise," and Richard L. Bushman's new "Yankee" of the prerevolutionary era. James A. Henretta's modern American of the revolutionary period is of the same bloodline.[4]

Recent historians of the American Revolution have built on this basic outlook by emphasizing that the contention and political mobilization of the revolutionary era further accustomed men to an individual, supralocal, activist, and optimistic political outlook. In Jackson Turner Main's *Political Parties Before the Constitution,* silent agrarians awake from deference into an active prosecution of their economic interests in the political arena. They succeed in attaining their ends. Gordon S. Wood is more subtle and, with others such as Rowland Berthoff and John M. Murrin, stresses the inadvertance of the whole process by which revolutionary Americans sought to restore the past and instead tumbled backward into modernity. But it is modernity into which they tumbled, the modernity of Jefferson's individualistic "yeoman freeholder" and of a society of coequal individuals bound by no

---

[3] Alex Inkeles and David H. Smith, *Becoming Modern: Individual Change in Six Developing Countries* (Cambridge: Harvard University Press, 1974), summarizes an extensive number of earlier articles by Inkeles.

[4] John A. Garraty, *The American Nation: A History of the United States,* 3rd ed. (New York: Harper & Row, 1975), pp. 30–31; Bernard Bailyn, *Education in the Forming of American Society: Needs and Opportunities for Study* (Chapel Hill: University of North Carolina Press, 1960), p. 49; Richard L. Bushman, *From Puritan to Yankee: Character and the Social Order in Connecticut, 1690–1765* (New York: W. W. Norton, 1970); James A. Henretta, *The Evolution of American Society, 1700–1815: An Interdisciplinary Analysis* (Lexington, Mass.: D. C. Heath, 1973).

tradition of hierarchical deference but only by those transitory "horizontal" associations of equals necessary to accomplish tasks too large for the liberated individual. As Richard D. Brown puts it, "it was during the American Revolution that the balance of traditional and modern elements in American society was decisively altered. Without generating any radical or spontaneous disruption of American society,[5] the political revolution provided overwhelming leverage for further modernization. Its impact was experienced . . . directly on the political structure and indirectly on social expectations and behavior." The result was "the modern personality." [6]

Historians of subsequent decades stretching into the nineteenth century take this new individual, liberated and transformed by social processes and by the Revolution, freed from traditional authorities down to and including his own parents, and they make him the basis for the good bourgeois citizen of a progressive middle-class society—a citizen practicing birth control because his education and mentality tell him this is practical and wise, living in short the model life of a model modern citizen, a thoroughly new man.[7]

[5] Most of those who link modernization with the American Revolution wish to envision the birth of the modern individual unaccompanied by serious social conflict or upheaval.

[6] Richard D. Brown, "Modernization and the Modern Personality in Early America, 1600–1865," *Journal of Interdisciplinary History*, 2 (1971–1972): 201–228. See also Jackson Turner Main, *Political Parties before the Constitution* (Chapel Hill: University of North Carolina Press, 1973); Gordon S. Wood, *The Creation of the American Republic, 1776–1787* (Chapel Hill: University of North Carolina Press, 1969); and subsequent unpublished papers on the social consequences of the Revolution delivered in 1975 and 1976 at various conferences on the American Revolution Bicentennial. Rowland Berthoff and John M. Murrin, "Feudalism, Communalism, and the Yeoman Freeholder: The American Revolution Considered as a Social Accident," pp. 256–288, in Stephen G. Kurtz and James H. Hutson, eds., *Essays on the American Revolution* (Chapel Hill: University of North Carolina Press, 1973).

[7] See, for example, Daniel Scott Smith, "Parental Power and Marriage Patterns: An Analysis of Historical Trends in Hingham, Massachusetts," *Journal of Marriage and the Family*, 35 (1973): 419–428; and Maris A. Vinovskis, "Socioeconomic Determinants of Interstate Fertility Differentials in the United States in 1850 and 1860," *Journal of Interdisciplinary History*, 6 (1975–1976): 375–396. Both Smith and Vinovskis fall explicitly or implicitly into the "Inkeles school" which assumes to

II. The Individual

How are we to regard this school of thought? Its essential feature is an emphasis on a nearly total psychic transformation as the key to the modern individual and on the modern individual as the key, or at least one major key, to social modernization. Such at least is the ultimate tendency of this line of interpretation, and in some ways, I am sympathetic to it. My own article contained hints of it, and my subsequent researches have turned up two pieces of evidence that such an individual was indeed evolving in early modern Anglo-America, even before the American Revolution. First, in New England and Virginia, as in England, persons who left wills were systematically refraining from the voluntary charitable contributions that had characterized a majority of the wills of all social classes in late medieval England. By the time of the Revolution, only 5% of testators bothered to leave such contributions. This is consistent with the idea of an emerging individual who withdraws from traditional social involvements, concentrating on his or her own family and interests and leaving wider social needs to voluntary organizations and to the state. Second, in the middle of the eighteenth century some of these same testators also began to write their wills ever further in advance of death, a possible indication of an increasing focus on planning and on rational calculation in the disposal of individual and of family property.[8] For some, then, behavior could have been

one degree or another changed attitudes and a changed personality. For Inkeles's own views on fertility, see *Becoming Modern* and (with Karen Miller), "Modernity and Acceptance of Family Limitation in Four Developing Countries," *Journal of Social Issues*, 30 (1974): 167–188.

[8] Both of these developments were discussed in my paper on "Attitudinal Modernization" delivered at the University of Edinburgh Conference on Anglo-American Society, June 1973. A copy of the paper and a letter annotating these points were sent to Daniel Scott Smith, who then raised one of these points in his 1975 review of my *Literacy in Colonial New England: An Enquiry into the Social Context of Literacy in the Early Modern West* (New York: W. W. Norton, 1974) in which he revealed an unawareness of the provenance of these two points. Smith also seems unaware that such forms of behavior were evinced by literate and illiterate people alike, and so only confirm the essential irrelevance of literacy to any such changes in attitudes—the latter was the thesis of *Literacy in Colonial New England.*

changing on a broad enough front to suggest possibly an entire new mentality of calculation and of rationality.

Within these limits, one could accept the idea of a transformation of the human personality, though I might add that this new personality, where and when it occurred, must be seen in a more sophisticated perspective than most writers on early American society are always willing to see it. It was not, indeed, peculiar to America but was in most aspects a Western phenomenon. Insofar as there was a new, modern man he could be found in many of his features earlier in England and soon enough in France.[9] Moreover, the evolution of any "modern personality" was almost surely inadvertant, through a process by which men, ironically, tried to restore the past in the face of new conditions, new experiences, and new attitudes. This, according to Gordon S. Wood and Rowland Berthoff and John M. Murrin, Robert A. Gross, and Harry Stout, is how modern man and his mass or "horizontal" society emerged from the initial, socially defensive behaviors of the American Revolution.[10] The change was inadvertant, as these authorities indicate. Finally, the modern individual, as first presented to us by Alexis de Tocqueville in the 1830s, is not necessarily to be viewed only as optimistic and enterprising—not by any means. Tocqueville invented the term "individualism" and here is how he described it:

As social conditions become more equal, the number of persons increases who, although they are neither rich nor powerful enough to exercise any great influence over their fellows, have nevertheless

[9] Again, see Wrigley, "Progress of Modernization," and also Emmanuel Le Roy Ladurie, *The Peasants of Languedoc,* trans. John Day (Urbana: University of Illinois Press, 1974). The specific mix of features in the hypothesized American modern personality may differ subtly from the mix hypothesized by Wrigley and implied by Le Roy Ladurie. Both may differ a bit from Inkeles's modern man as derived from research in today's developing nations, but the common features are most impressive and appear to justify considering the hypothesized modern personality as a Western and, perhaps, universal phenomenon.

[10] Wood, *Creation of the American Republic;* Berthoff and Murrin, "Feudalism, Communalism, and the Yeoman Freeholder"; Robert A. Gross, *The Minutemen and Their World* (New York: Hill and Wang, 1976); and Harry Stout, "Religion, Communications, and the Ideological Origins of the Revolution" (unpublished paper, 1976).

acquired or retained sufficient education and fortune to satisfy their own wants. They owe nothing to any man, they expect nothing from any man; they acquire the habit of always considering themselves as standing alone, and they are apt to imagine that their whole destiny is in their own hands. [These men are individualists.] Individualism is a mature and calm feeling, which disposes each member of the communty to sever himself from the mass of his fellows, and to draw apart with his family and his friends; so that, after he has thus formed a little circle of his own, he willingly leaves society at large to itself. Thus, not only does democracy make every man forget his ancestors, but it hides his descendants and separates his contemporaries from him; it throws him back forever upon himself alone, and threatens in the end to confine him entirely within the solitude of his own heart.[11]

The Marxists would have us believe that this troubled modern individual is a product of bourgeois capitalist society, rather than of modern Western society in general, and that he is a hopelessly warped product of a warped system. They have only to look to the satellite states of the Soviet Union to see that modern man is a Western or European creature who emerges under all systems. And this universal modern man, withdrawn into the solitude of his own life, family, and heart, does have problems of identity, as Tocqueville suggested. The problem is put in a beautifully balanced perspective by the American novelist, James Agee, describing life in an early twentieth-century American family:

> On the rough wet grass of the back yard my father and mother have spread quilts. We all lie there, my mother, my father, my uncle, my aunt, and I too am lying there. . . . They are not talking much, and the talk is quiet, of nothing in particular, of nothing at all in particular, of nothing at all. The stars are wide and alive, they seem each like a smile of great sweetness, and they seem very near. All my people are larger bodies than mine . . . with voices gentle and meaningless like the voices of sleeping birds. One is an artist, he is living at home. One is a musician, she is living at home. One is my mother who is good to me. One is my father who is good to me. By some chance, here they are, all on this earth; and who shall ever tell the sorrow of being on this earth, lying, on quilts, on the grass, in a summer evening, among the sounds of night. May God bless my people, my uncle, my aunt,

---

[11] Alexis de Tocqueville, *Democracy in America: Part the Second, The Social Influence of Democracy*, trans. Henry Reeve (New York: J. and H. G. Langley, 1840), Book 2, Chapter 2.

my mother, my good father, oh, remember them kindly in their time of trouble; and in the hour of their taking away.

After a little while, I am taken in and put to bed. Sleep, soft smiling, draws me unto her: and those receive me, who quietly treat me, as one familiar and well-beloved in that home: but will not, oh, will not, not now, not ever; but will not ever tell me who I am.[12]

For this individual, in the sanctity of a small circle of family, the problem is identity. And such identity as modern man has is that of a liberated individual whose personality is characterized by self-control. We can see this in the poignant modern individuals described in the works of Daniel Scott Smith, Maris Vinovskis, and Alex Inkeles—modern individuals, their attitudes transformed by circumstances and education, determined to increase the affluence of their families by limiting the number of births.[13] Clearly this personality is not an unmixed blessing.

III. Social Change and Human Personality

But was there such a personality in the first place? Did an individualistic, rational, calculating, planning, instrumental man, moving with his family through a horizontal, mass society really emerge in Western society, before, in the course of, and after the American Revolution? This is the larger question which arises from the current literature on the American Revolution and modernization and from the wider literature on modernization in the early modern West. It is an essential question. For, whatever the structural aspects of any modernization which occurred, we are speaking of an entire transformation of the human personality in the recent course of Western history.

It seems to me that the evidence available from American and from other Western societies in the eighteenth and nineteenth

12 James Agee, *A Death in the Family* (New York: McDowell, Obolensky, 1957), pp. 7–8. Copyright 1957 by the James Agee Trust. Used with permission.

13 See also Stout, "Religion, Communications, and Ideological Origins," for this same awareness of the liabilities of any new personality. For the works by Smith, Vinovskis, and Inkeles, see notes 3 and 7.

centuries permits us simultaneously to take a much more limited view of the whole impact of social change on the human personality. Let me take one example, the voluntary organization. Under the assumptions of the "modern personality" school, the voluntary organization is only a transitory, horizontal association of equals created to accomplish a specific functional task which cannot be accomplished by one individual. Once the task is carried out, the modern individuals go their own ways without further allegiance. Thus, a street-paving association or a local militia organization does its job and is no more. Even in this form, as Tocqueville observed, the voluntary organization is the one force which can unite individuals for effective action and so remove them from isolation and give them a sense of effectiveness vis-à-vis the overwhelming tides of majority opinion and the immense power of the nation–state. Still, the evidence is that the voluntary organizations that sprang up like wild grass in the decades after the American Revolution served far more varied and covert functions than even Tocqueville realized. To take only one instance, the Adrian, Michigan, Guards was last and least a militia unit. It was more a means of identifying and reinforcing the hierarchy of wealth, status, and leadership in this new town, of absorbing recent arrivals into the mutual relations which pervaded this hierarchy, and of binding all together in certain common feelings, assumptions, and ceremonies. While in some towns such organizations were several and separate, in most towns they overlapped considerably, and in early Adrian there was essentially only one. Regardless, what such voluntary organizations represented was the adoption of new tactics in order to reconstruct the social and emotional realities of a stable community under the changing structural circumstances of a mobile and developing America. To the extent that this effort succeeded, what we have underneath is a homeostatic human personality, adapting its constant end (community) to changed circumstances (mobility) through the adoption of new tactical behaviors (such as voluntary organizations). The question arises, how many new tactical behaviors can this human personality adopt and still remain in large part constant? The answer might be, many more and to a much larger degree for much longer than has been thought.

KENNETH A. LOCKRIDGE

Admittedly, at this point we need a theory of the personality to clarify the issues involved. For virtually no historian has offered a clear definition or theory of the human personality to buttress claims for or against cumulative personality change. The modernists seem to believe that behavior is equivalent to personality. They imply that when behavior and the associated culture undergo substantial change, this signifies a change in personality. Perhaps, but an amazing amount of behavior and an unrecognized proportion of culture remain essentially constant through long spans of time. And the family context, which does so much to shape the human personality, has changed only in subtle and contradictory ways over the centuries of supposed modernization of the personality. Beneath all this, lies the evidence of certain constant human motives and of the homeostatic capacity to adopt new tactical behaviors to keep these motives and the ends they imply constant: community, a share of perceived resources, and security. Surely this is not so obvious that we can ignore it in constructing a total view of the Western personality in the course of centuries of structural change.

Although no adequate theory of the human personality or of its changes has been used to support the historians of the modernization school, and although I can offer no such total theory to confirm my own skepticism about the degree of personality change in the process of modernization, I can turn for help to the work of Charles Tilly. Tilly is no theoretician of the personality; he is a student of such things as the decline in fertility and the rise of formal education in early modern Europe, and above all of the changing levels and forms of collective action, particularly collective violence and strikes, in the eighteenth- and nineteenth-century West. Tilly's scholarship, together with some unpublished manuscripts, coming as it does from an evidential perspective entirely different from the works on revolutionary America, offers an essentially homeostatic view of the human personality in an era of social change. Tilly stoutly resists positing a new or transformed human personality. His work is significant for all of us struggling with this problem.

For example, consider the decline in fertility and rise in formal education which began among bourgeois households in

112

THE AMERICAN REVOLUTION, MODERNIZATION, AND MAN

seventeenth- and eighteenth-century France and which spread to most of Western society in the nineteenth century. Tilly explains these changes in terms of a constant human personality marked by a desire to be cared for in old age. This personality initially adopts the tactic of high fertility, hoping that a few of the many children born will survive into adulthood, marry, and prosper, thereby providing old-age insurance. Under certain conditions, a sudden fall in infant mortality persuades this person to adopt a new tactic: Fertility is lowered and fewer children conceived because it is more probable that they will survive to adulthood. The investment of resources which formerly went into conceiving and feeding many fragile children now goes into educating a few sturdy children in formal schools, with the hope that these educated children will provide old-age insurance. This is a simplification of a speculative argument, but one can see that Tilly does tend to assume a constant underlying personality with continuing goals, adopting new fertility and investment tactics in the face of altered structural conditions.[14]

The difference between Professor Tilly and such other students of changed fertility behavior as Maris Vinovskis, Daniel Scott Smith, and Alex Inkeles can be drawn out by means of a diagram which Tilly himself has used in a forthcoming review of a book on the evolving modern personality by Alex Inkeles. Basically, Inkeles and the others regard lowered fertility and all other "modern" behaviors as the products of a process which looks like this:

Social Conditions → Type of Learning → Attitudes → Behavior → [Personality]

The implication is that changed structural conditions create new "learning environments," among them schools, in which the lessons of the new social environment are learned, lessons which alter attitudes and ultimately the whole personality, and finally change behavior. Thus, improved social and economic prospects are conveyed *via* schools and labor unions, altering the personality

---

[14] Charles Tilly, "Population and Pedagogy in France," *History of Education Quarterly*, 13 (1973): 113–128. See also, Charles Tilly, ed., *Historical Studies of Changing Fertility* (forthcoming).

in the direction of a belief in rational planning and progress, resulting in decisions to control fertility in order to get ahead. In this instance, to focus the example further, literacy could be a useful intervening variable in the process leading through new types of learning to a new personality and to lower fertility.[15] Tilly suggests a very different diagram of causation:

Social Conditions → Type of Learning

$\downarrow$ $\qquad\qquad$ $\downarrow$ $\qquad$ [Personality?]

Behavior $\qquad\qquad$ Attitudes

Again, to take the specific example of lower fertility, Tilly's explanation would be that fertility limitation is a specific tactical behavior designed to preserve constant goals under changed conditions of child mortality. Whether wider learning or changed attitudes or changed personality ensues is not only problematic but in fact unnecessary and possibly even unlikely. Incidentally, in Tilly's scheme literacy would therefore have a lessened role, appearing possibly as a useful tool in learning how to control fertility, and certainly as an indirect result of the larger investment in children's education, but not necessarily an intimate part of a linear process which first educates, then changes attitudes, and then alters the human personality and so leads to controlled fertility. In fact, to Tilly, literacy becomes chiefly an epiphenomenon in a continuous struggle for human adequacy in the face of changing structural conditions.

Some of these points can be seen more clearly though in a more implicit form in Tilly's work on collective violence in eighteenth- and nineteenth-century Europe.[16] For fertility and education are not his home ground and, as he says, "if there is a Grail (of social change) I expect to find it in changing class structure and power relations." In this area, Tilly has explicitly

[15] Charles Tilly, "Talking Modern" (review of Inkeles and Smith, *Becoming Modern*), *Peasant Studies Newsletter*, forthcoming.

[16] Charles Tilly, "The Modernization of Political Conflict in France," in Edward B. Harvey, ed., *Perspectives on Modernization: Essays in Memory of Ian Weinberg* (Toronto: University of Toronto Press, 1972). A massive body of subsequent research is summarized and theoretical implications are drawn out in Charles Tilly, *From Mobilization to Revolution* (forthcoming).

thrown away "the blurry word, modernization" except as a set of specific structural changes. Most prominent among these are the rise of the all-powerful nation–state and the formation of new power relations between that state and corporate industrial powers on the one hand and the peasant or worker on the other hand. The consequence of these changes and of these new relationships is not an anxious, future-shocked, and violent modern personality. Nothing of the sort. The consequences revealed by Tilly's researches can be summed up as follows: Between, say, 1600 and 1825, reactive forms of collective action and of strikes and violence predominated, as social groups resisted the encroaching claims of the state and of market forces on all areas of their lives; by the middle nineteenth century the state and large corporations had succeeded in nearly monopolizing social resources, and so they became targets for "proactive" collective actions in which social groups made new claims, claims aimed at bettering their position in relation to those extremely powerful organizations; the result was not any particular increase in the level of collective violence, so much as a shift in the aims, forms, and tactics of collective action and of its natural extension, collective violence. Local protests over taxes or over food prices, and tax and food riots, gave way to the organized interest group seeking to gain its aims by parliamentary elections, by lobbying, by mass meetings and demonstrations, by marches, and at times by new forms of violence. Partly as a consequence of the new goals and forms of collective organization, the number of strikes did increase and these tended to become large, dramatic, and brief—public, one might say. But the increase in strikes is not as significant as the overall change in the forms of action.

This icy, objective portrait of modernization and of human change speaks not a word of a new personality, and we know from Tilly's other work of his skepticism on this count. Men faced changing structural circumstances, he seems to be saying, and so they changed their tactics and, in a limited sense, their goals. But beneath it all runs the distinct impression of a constant man adapting himself to changed power relations in order to preserve his interests in a world of structural forces essentially outside of his control. Tactics change, but does man?

Tilly's contribution amounts more to a query than an answer, but in the context of the existing literature, it is an exceedingly important query. And we can see Tilly's implicit skepticism dramatically juxtaposed with the more cataclysmic modernization literature in the specific case of the American Revolution. For, where others have looked at the Revolution and seen the multiple origins of an utterly new "modern" personality, Tilly, in his essay in this volume, takes a more limited approach.[17] He seems to be saying that the Revolution was a sort of pressure cooker, in which the colonists quickly and of necessity shifted from old forms of collective action—the tax and food riots so characteristic of eighteenth-century society—to such new forms as the association, the strike or boycott, the demonstration, and the committee of correspondence. These forms were simultaneously emerging among the radicals in London and would be the characteristic forms of collective action in the nineteenth century.

It is difficult to predict how far Tilly might take the implications of his view of these revolutionary tactics in America. On the one hand, he seems to be saying that the level of mobilization and of effectiveness of these new forms of action became so high in the colonies that a true revolution emerged and the collective associations in fact became a new government. How revolutionary the ultimate implications of this event were, however, is another matter, and Tilly's own work may set the limit. For modern America seems to emerge in Tilly's larger view rather like modern Europe, as yet another society dominated by the state and by large corporations, in which groups continued pressing their "proactive" claims by means of the forms of action first perfected in the Revolution. And in no case does Tilly speak of the Revolution, any more than he does of any other event or events, as the source of an utterly new human personality.

I think we must agree that the issue is open. One body of evidence, which draws in part upon the experiences of the American Revolution, suggests that a new, modern personality evolved. In this view, mankind may also be more anxious and more controlled and is certainly cut off from mankind in the past. Under another

[17] Chapter 3 of this volume.

view, we are descendants of the Revolution merely in the sense that we are now the latest participants in a tactical struggle for human adequacy in the face of structural changes largely beyond our control. This view has its benefits, however, for some of our latest tactics seem to be as effective as those employed in the past, and we are in general more closely linked with our fellows in the past.

It is all very well to say that reality must lie between these interpretative ideal types of man. For the moment, these are the ideal types we are presented with. Each has implications for the way we view the American Revolution, or voluntary organizations, or literacy or fertility. Each has implications for psycho-history, too, since the former view suggests that a psychological discipline based on twentieth-century man cannot be applied to an understanding of man in the past, while the latter view shows less hesitancy on this score.[18] And, before the synthesizers begin their work, let me say that I am inclined to the view which keeps us closer to the past, simply because I find it more comforting.

In a more moderate perspective, Charles Tilly's work and a little common sense in the matter of "personality" are useful levers on a serious scholarly question: How different are we from humankind in the past? Tilly's view is, of course, almost too basic, and tends toward truism. There is a sense in which he says nothing more than that men are born, breed, breathe, struggle, and die; and what is that to say? What I am suggesting, and what is also implicit in Tilly's work, is that there may be more. Particularly the idea of homeostatic man, adapting constant ends to new circumstances through changed behaviors, enrolls much of constancy in a more sophisticated conception of the processes of human change. If Tocqueville's voluntary associations, such as the Adrian Guard, are not what they seem, then neither is man nor entirely are his changes. If forms of collective action have been

18 Thus, while a skeptical view of the modernization of the human person-ality checks some of the excesses of some psychohistorians, it rewards them with a less restricted understanding of the human personality in the past.

adaptations to a constant struggle for resources, this too may involve something more than truism. More, if the family context has not changed strongly, or has altered cyclically, then quite complex structures of the human personality are likely to have endured intact, or recurred. The real and symbolic apparati adopted by this personality are all we can study, yet we are faced with the paradox that these may express significant commonalities we cannot reach or have not tried to.

A more poignant expression of the problem lies in Egil Johansson's idea of the toy box. Perhaps, says this Swedish scholar, there has been little change in human manipulativeness and possibly in other important properties over the last 500 years or more. As he puts it, the mental toy box of mankind was as full 300 years ago as it is today, only the objects have changed. Can we then speak of a more manipulative or rational or intelligent modern man? The "toy box" is yet another lever in the effort to construct a metaphor of the personality by which we can recognize the persistence of man in the midst of contrapuntal changes.

What is needed is not truism but a refined sense of (or sense of refined) continuities, and of cyclicities, so multifarious, and in so strange conjunctures with linear changes obvious and subtle, that in fact a whole new metaphor of social process is called forth. Can we say that consciousness, for example, develops only linearly? That I think would be a statement which reflects the smug conceit of the modern era. Or if we leave aside personality, shall we speak only linearly of humankind's notions of what a person is or ought to be, as these nations have arisen variously in the multifarity of cultures and times across the vast span of human history? This claim ignores the very resonances across culture and across time which are the humanities as we have known them. What is needed, too, is a sense of man which, if it does not penetrate to the personality, comes closer; a definition of man more conscious and subtle than the usual search for behavioral changes. I cannot prescribe this, only envision it.[19]

---

[19] For a fine example of what is needed, see James A. Henretta, "*Mentalité* in Pre-industrial America: Family Values and Agricultural Production," *William and Mary Quarterly* (forthcoming).

THE AMERICAN REVOLUTION, MODERNIZATION, AND MAN

At issue finally is the whig metaphor which has dominated Western history for the past 200 years. "Modernization" is sometimes simply this metaphor in scientific disguise. Partly true, this metaphor is also profoundly chauvinistic and, in its final view of man, isolating. It isolates "modern" men from the past and likewise from one another. Certainly in the United States, the modern personality and the partly arbitrary myth of such a personality, armed with the revolutionary legacy of individual rights, have been characterized by a savage disregard of all human commonality. The first step in reviving a sense of our common humanity, toward one another and toward others abroad, might be a scholarly recognition of that humanity which we have carried with us all along. This would be no betrayal of a Revolution whose most important inheritance has been a desire to deepen its own legacy.

Index

Marion, Francis, 19
Marshall, John, 19
Martin, James K., 90
Marxists, 109
Maryland, 81, 89
Mason, George, 31, 98
Massachusetts, 5, 17, 21, 26, 51, 59, 67–70, 81, 83, 84, 88, 91, 96, *see also* Shays Rebellion
protests against British policy, 60–65, *see also* Intolerable Acts, protest against in Massachusetts; Stamp Act, riot against in Boston
Massachusetts Regulators, *see* Shays Rebellion
Mayor, Lord, London, 58, 60
Middle-Class Democracy and the Revolution . . ., by Robert E. Brown, 37
Minute Boys of New York City, The, by James Otis Kaler, 32
Minutemen, 40
Mississippi River, 97
Missouri, 14
Modernization, 9, 110, 115, *see also* Tilly, Charles
American Revolution and, 104–107, 116
personality and, 103–104, 118–119
scholarly views on, 104
voluntary organizations and, 111
Monticello, Va., 20
Morefields, London, 55
Morgan, Edmund S., 6, 81
Morgan, Helen M., 6
Morris, Robert, 98
Morris, Robert Hunter, 83
Morse, Jedidiah, 20
Mount Vernon, Va., 23
Munro, John, 85
Munroe, Samuel, 88
Murrin, John M., 105, 108

N

Namier, Lewis B., 2–3, 5
Nash, Gary B., 74
Nashville, Tenn., 97

National Intelligencer, Daily, 23
"Nature," by Ralph Waldo Emerson, 14
"Nature of American Loyalism," by Leonard Labaree, 37
Naval Academy, U.S., 32
Nelson, William, 36–37
Neville, John, 86
Neville, Samuel, 85
Newark Daily Advertiser, 30
New England, 15, 28, 31, 78, 81, 107
New Hamiltonians, 34
New Hampshire, 83
New Jersey, 78, 81, 83, 84, 85, 86, 88, *see also* New Jersey antiproprietary land rioters
New Jersey antiproprietary land rioters, 79, 81, 83, 85, 86, 88, 92, 95
New Palace Yard, London, 54
New York, 5, 81, 83, 84, 85, 86, 87, 88, 92, *see also* New York antirent rioters
New York antirent rioters, 79, 81, 85, 86, 88, 92, 94, 96
Nichols, William, 86
Niles, Hezekiah, 20, 25
North, Frederick (Lord North), 40, 69
North, Lord, *see* North, Frederick
North American Review, 25
North Briton, ed. John Wilkes, 54
North Carolina, 57, 81, 84, 85, 89, 93, 94, 97, 98, *see also* Regulators, North Carolina
North Carolina Regulators, *see* Regulators, North Carolina
North End, Boston, Mass., 62–63
Northern Neck, Va., 81
Northwest, Old, 98
Nottingham, 52

O

Ohio River, 23
Old Manse, Concord, Mass., 14
Old Northwest, *see* Northwest, Old
Old Southwest, *see* Southwest, Old
Oliver, Andrew, 63
Onion River Land Co. 87

126

Ordeal of Thomas Hutchinson, The, by
Bernard Bailyn, 4
Origins of American Politics, by
Bernard Bailyn, 4
Otis, James, 19
Ourstory, 41

P

Pacific coast, 23
Paine, Thomas, 14, 37
Palfrey, John Gorham, 31
Palmer, Robert R., 7, 71
Pandours, 79
Panton, Vt., 84
Paris, 13, 32, 40
Parker, Theodore, 29
Parkman, Francis, 31
Parliament, 46, 54, 56, 57–58, 59, 60, 63, 71
Parrington, Vernon L., 2, 3
Patrick Henry, by William Wirt, 19, 25
Paulding, James Kirke, 19
*Paul Revere and the World He Lived
in,* by Esther Forbes, 35
Paxton Boys uprising, 80, 82, 83, 86, 89, 92, 93, 94, 95
Paxton Township, Pa., 82
Pelham, Mass., 88
Pennamite, *see* Yankee–Pennamite
conflict
Pennsylvania, 23, 81, 84, 86, 89, 93, 95, 98, *see also* Fries Rebellion; Paxton
Boys uprising; Whiskey Rebellion
People's Bicentennial Commission, 7
Personality, human, *see also* Inkeles,
Alex; Modernization; Tilly, Charles
American Revolution and, 105–106, 108
social change and, 111–119
Petersham, Mass., 95
Peterson, Merrill, 34
Petition of Right, 40
Philadelphia, Pa., 16, 21, 33, 39, 83
Philip II, King of Spain, 22
Philips family, 85
Pictorial Field Book of the Revolution,
by Benson J. Lossing, 28
Pitkin, Timothy, 19

Pitt, William the elder, 3
Planter's Adventure, ship, 67
Plymouth, Mass., 64
Pocock, J. G. A., 4
Political Parties Before the Constitution,
by Jackson Turner Main, 105
Pontiac's War, 82
Pope, Barnaby, 89
Pope's Day, 68
Population, *see* Land–population–
wealth crisis in eighteenth-century
America
Portsmouth, Eng., 57
Postmaster, Charleston, S.C., 69
Pound, Ezra, 34
Powell, Sumner Chilton, 77
Pre-emption law, 98–99
Prendergast, William, 88, 91
Prescott, William Hickling, 22
Prince Georges County, Maryland, 32
Principles and Acts of the Revolution,
ed. Hezekiah Niles, 25
Proprietors, East Jersey, 83, 85, 92, 95,
see also New Jersey antiproprietary
land rioters
*Prospectus for the "Common School
Journal",* by Horace Mann, 15
Protestant Cemetery, Paris, 32
Puritan tradition, 15

Q

Quakers, 83
Quebec Act, 58, 59

R

"Racial Equality in America," by John
Hope Franklin, 41
Ramsay, David, 19, 33
Randall, Henry, 19
Randolph, John of Roanoke, 39
Rantoul, Robert, Jr., 26
Rebellions, American back country,
1740–1799
activity patterns, 91–95
antilegal nature, 92–94

127

Rebellions, *(cont.)*
defensive nature, 94–95
enemies of rebels, 82–86
goals, 82
grievances of rebels, 81–82
leadership patterns, 86–91
length of rebellions, 86
listed (nine), 79–80
number of participants, 73
success or failure, 95–96
waning of, 97–99
Rebels and Democrats . . ., by Elijah
P. Douglass, 2
Reconstruction, Southern, 15
Reed, William B., 25
Regulators, Massachusetts, *see* Shays
Rebellion
Regulators, North Carolina, 80–81, 83,
85, 86, 89–90, 93, 94, 95, 96
Regulators, South Carolina, 66, 80, 82,
83, 84, 86, 89, 90, 92, 93, 94, 95, 96
Reid, John, 83
Renaissance, Italian, 4
Representatives, House of, 21
Revolution, American, *see also* Adams,
John; Bancroft, George; Fisher,
Sydney George; Force, Peter; Jef-
fersonian Republicans; Lossing,
Benson J.; Madison, James; Rush,
Benjamin; Sabine, Lorenzo; Simms,
William Gilmore
Bicentennial, 41
Centennial, 29–31
collective actions, 71–72
conservative view of, 17, 31, 35–39
contemporary views of, 16–18, 39
democracy reaffirmed in re,. 34–35
1832 and, 22–23
1875–1906 period, views on, 29–32, 39
elites and, 35–37, *see also* Revolutionaries, American
ideology of, 1–4, 75
impact on human history, 26
intellectual legacy, 4–7
legacy threatened, 25–26
literary history, 32
local historians of, 31
middle nineteenth-century views on,
24–29, 39

middle twentieth-century views on,
35–38, 39
modernization and, 1, 9–10
narrative histories of, 19–20
1907–1944 period, views on, 33–35,
39
personality, human, and, 10
present mindedness and, 13–14
realism on human nature and, 35,
37–38
scholars versus popularizers of, 34, 41
social change and, 16–18, 40
social conflict and, 1–2, 5–9, 73
tradition, national, and 4–5, 14–16,
40, 13–41 *passim*
Revolution, Atlantic, 50
Revolution, Chinese, 7, 71–72
Revolution, Europe, 1848, 72
Revolution, French, 7, 17, 71–72
Revolution, Russian, 7, 71–72
Revolutionaries, American, *see* also
Revolution, American
biographies of, 18–19
reburials of, 32
romanticized and immortalized,
18–23, 39
sons of, 25
Revolutionary War, 81
Rhode Island, 5
Rights, English and American, local
defense of, 52–54
Rioters, *see* New Jersey antiproprietary
land rioters; New York antirent
rioters; Riots
Riots, 53–54, *see also* Rioters
food, 52–53
Robbins, Caroline, 3
Roberts, Amos, 88, 91
Robinson Crusoe, by Daniel Defoe, 18
Roche, John, 37
Rocky Mountains, 23
Rodrock, John, 86
Roosevelt, Franklin D., 86
Roots, by Alex Haley, 41
Rossiter, Clinton, 3
Royal Exchange, London, 58
Rudé, George, 9, 48–49
Rush, Benjamin, 7, 15
on American Revolution, 16–17

A	
B	7
C	8
D	9
E	0
F	1
G	2
H	3
I	4
J	5

STUDIES IN SOCIAL DISCONTINUITY

Under the Consulting Editorship of:

CHARLES TILLY   EDWARD SHORTER
University of Michigan   University of Toronto

William A. Christian, Jr. Person and God in a Spanish Valley

Joel Samaha. Law and Order in Historical Perspective: The Case of Elizabethan Essex

John W. Cole and Eric R. Wolf. The Hidden Frontier: Ecology and Ethnicity in an Alpine Valley

Immanuel Wallerstein. The Modern World-System: Capitalist Agriculture and the Origins of the European World-Economy in the Sixteenth Century

John R. Gillis. Youth and History: Tradition and Change in European Age Relations 1770 – Present

D. E. H. Russell. Rebellion, Revolution, and Armed Force: A Comparative Study of Fifteen Countries with Special Emphasis on Cuba and South Africa

Kristian Hvidt. Flight to America: The Social Background of 300,000 Danish Emigrants

James Lang. Conquest and Commerce: Spain and England in the Americas

Stanley H. Brandes. Migration, Kinship, and Community: Tradition and Transition in a Spanish Village

Daniel Chirot. Social Change in a Peripheral Society: The Creation of a Balkan Colony

Jane Schneider and Peter Schneider. Culture and Political Economy in Western Sicily

Michael Schwartz. Radical Protest and Social Structure: The Southern Farmers' Alliance and Cotton Tenancy, 1880-1890

Ronald Demos Lee (Ed.). Population Patterns in the Past

David Levine. Family Formations in an Age of Nascent Capitalism

Dirk Hoerder. Crowd Action in Revolutionary Massachusetts, 1765-1780

Charles P. Cell. Revolution at Work: Mobilization Campaigns in China

Frederic L. Pryor. The Origins of the Economy: A Comparative Study of Distribution in Primitive and Peasant Economies

Harry W. Pearson. The Livelihood of Man by Karl Polanyi

Richard Maxwell Brown and Don E. Fehrenbacher (Eds.). Tradition, Conflict, and Modernization: Perspectives on the American Revolution

In preparation

Juan Guillermo Espinosa and Andrew S. Zimbalist. Economic Democracy: Workers' Participation in Chilean Industry, 1970-1973

Randolph Trumbach. The Rise of the Egalitarian Family: Aristocratic Kinship and Domestic Relations in Eighteenth-Century England

Arthur L. Stinchcombe. Theoretical Methods in Social History